Fast Forward Your Career

 7 Career Success Principles

RICHARD E. HINKIE

Copyright © 2013 by Richard E. Hinkie

First Edition – November 2013

ISBN

978-1-4602-1748-1 (Hardcover)

978-1-4602-1749-8 (Paperback)

978-1-4602-1750-4 (eBook)

Produced by:

FriesenPress

Suite 300 – 852 Fort Street

Victoria, BC, Canada V8W 1H8

www.friesenpress.com

Distributed to the trade by The Ingram Book Company

"The journey of a thousand miles begins with a single step." Lau Tzu

Your career journey also begins with a single step, but along the way you will take many more steps. Will they be productive? Will they lead to career success and satisfaction? Will you be passive, or will you take charge of your career direction? Because you are a unique individual, your career journey can only be your own, but you can benefit from the wisdom of others. In this book, successful people have unselfishly shared their career success principles. Use their guidance regularly as you take each step in your journey.

"The Serenity Prayer" has helped millions of people let go of distractions and take responsibility for their lives.

Here is my version of the "Serenity Prayer," as it relates to careers.

Grant me the serenity to let go of the expectation that others will move my career forward,

The courage to take proactive action for my own future development,

And the wisdom to know that I can make a unique, positive contribution in my career.

Ric Hinkie

Table of Contents

Fast Forward Your Career

7 Career Success Principles

RICHARD E. HINKIE

DEDICATION

This book is dedicated to every employee and entrepreneur who has both the passion and the willingness to take action to consistently grow his or her knowledge and skills to make a positive difference at work; for the organization, the community, and the world at large.

In my life and work experience, the following people exemplified these principles: Berniece Norma Hinkie, Bradley G. Morrison, Charles Applequist, John Golle, Phil Mahla, Steve Ewing, Jeff Yundt, and Bill Herdegen.

ACKNOWLEDGMENTS

Without the unselfish and thoughtful sharing by more than 60 executives about their career journey, from new hire to senior executive, there wouldn't be any worthwhile content on these pages. The "how did you get where you are" interview series began with executives from energy companies, thanks to Patrick Van Beek, president of the Midwest Energy Association and publisher of each individual interview over the last six years. To their wisdom about what it takes to achieve career success, I was able to add insights from executives in government, from Apple and other technology companies, as well as retail, marketing, manufacturing, service and other industries.

The work of conducting the interviews, comparing what worked for each executive and developing the 7 Principles of Career Success is now complete. There are several "volunteers" who greatly assisted me in producing a better book. The portion of the manuscript that reflects proper use of the English language is due in large measure to my friend and neighbor Russell Klauk, a retired linguistics professor and to Carole Mathewson, copy editor. The organization and special content additions came from two very special people in my life: my brother Mark Hinkie, retired

President/COO of Pella Engineered Products, and one of the most accomplished developers of people and business relationships I have ever known, and Len Lampert, Harvard-educated architect, entrepreneur and friend of over 50 years. Joe Eastman, successful HR executive, customer-service executive, and career coach; Tim Burke, vice president of Omaha Public Power; John Golle, CEO and entrepreneur of numerous enterprises; and Scott Miller, CEO of the Holmes Corporation were also especially generous with their reviews and suggestions.

If there are errors, omissions or a failure to communicate, I am solely responsible. The wisdom on these pages comes from a group of unique individuals with a common purpose, to help you make the most of your career. I believe that you, the reader, will find the information and the career lessons universal.

Ric Hinkie

INTRODUCTION

For seven years, I have been interviewing successful business people every month. Among my first questions are always, "How did you get promoted ahead of other people? What separated you from the pack?" Each interviewee answered these questions and shared personal stories about his or her career success with me. All of the interviewees also provided real-life examples of how they moved forward in their careers. Every month, the most recent interview was published in a national industry journal.

The more interviews I did, the more I began to notice common themes. There seemed to be consistent patterns as to how these successful people moved forward in their careers.

As my own retirement, grew closer, the patterns I was seeing in the interviews caused me to think about my own career progression. How did I get where I was? What decisions did I make along the way that helped me grow from an entry-level position as a communications writer to become president of an organization that serves most of the gas and electric companies and their tens of thousands of employees in the United States? Did my career follow some of the same patterns that the successful people I interviewed did?

I wondered if the common patterns or principles of success would continue to be present in interviews with executives from a wider variety of industries. No matter with whom I talked, from the former vice president of Apple Stores to a retired United States Surgeon General, in interview after interview, one or more of the success principles I uncovered was also part of each person's career success.

When I reread and mind mapped all 60 completed executive interviews, I was struck by how consistently the same set of common career-success principles appeared. It was like looking at the night sky. Instead of seeing only individual stars (like the individual interviews I had completed), I was also seeing patterns (the common success principles from the interviews), like constellations in the night sky. The more I reread and compared interviews, the more a set of career-success principles emerged.

The next question for me was, "Would gathering and sharing these career-success principles be of value to readers like you, whether you are just beginning your work life, or are now ready to advance your career to the next level?"

I hope you will agree, after reading this book, the answer is "yes," you can apply these career-success principles to your own work life and get the job satisfaction, promotions and income you deserve faster. Go ahead, Fast Forward Your Career!

Of course, the exact experiences and details of every successful person's career are different, just as yours will be. But the sooner you understand and apply the proven, successful principles the executives I interviewed used in their careers, the faster you can move ahead in yours.

Whether you realize it or not, you have your own professional career "brand." (If you are not a marketing person familiar with branding, then think of the word "reputation" instead.)

Brand is a marketing term that describes how customers, investors, and others see a product, company, or a person. Mercedes Benz has a very different brand than Subaru. Both companies make automobiles, but they are different companies with carefully crafted brands designed to appeal to different types of customers. Individuals have a professional brand too. Oprah Winfrey's brand is empathetic, highly professional, and human. Donald Trump's brand is tough, opinionated, and impatient.

Your Facebook page is an example of your *personal* brand. In your career, however, your future depends a great deal on how your *professional* brand is perceived within the organizations you work for.

Whether you think of your reputation and image in your organization as your brand or not, your co-workers, your boss, your boss' boss, customers, and others whom you are in contact with, all have their view of who you are. In effect, that is your professional brand.

One of your first challenges in your career progression is to establish your professional brand so that people know who you are. Obviously, you want your brand to be well thought of. This process of creating your initial professional brand is covered in this book under the first major section, labeled **Level 1: Establish Your Brand**. There are three career success principles that apply at this level: *1. Get Connected and Get Noticed, No One Gets Ahead Without Help, 2. Be a Star Where You Are: Future Promotions Begin with Success in Your Current Job, and 3. Know Yourself & What You Want: Create Your Own Unique Career Plan.*

Level 2: Build Your Brand is the part of the book that explains the other four Career Success Principles.

Fast Forward 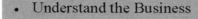 Your Career

Level 1: Establish Your Brand

- Get Connected & Get Noticed
- Be a Star Where You Are
- Know Yourself & What You Want

Level 2: Build Your Brand

- Understand the Business
- Be Ready
- Grow as a Leader
- Never Say Never

Make Your Plan and Work It: Update Regularly

Here is how the two major sections of the book work together. The arrows on the side will help remind you that applying the 7 Principles of Career Success is always an ongoing process. At each new level in your career you may need to apply a principle in a new way. For example, a senior manager may need to **Get Connected and Get Noticed** by corporate officers from divisions all across the company. Those types of connections are at a higher level than those needed by a new first-line supervisor who needs to become known around his own department and division.

Don't Be Intimidated by the Interviewees' Success

This isn't a book about superstar CEOs. The 7 Principles of Career Success uncovered in the research for this book apply at all career levels.

Don't be intimidated by the level of the people I interviewed. Each began his or her career in an entry-level job, just as you probably did. Some had little or no college education. Others began as specialists or individual contributors in IT, HR, engineering or accounting. Still others began in retail, sales, customer service or in "hands-on" field work. All of the interviewees competed with their peers and had to balance job, family, and personal challenges, just as you do. One executive began his career shoveling coal, and another was an electric meter reader. Today, both are corporate officers.

Somehow, all of the executives I interviewed were promoted faster and more often than their peers. Most admitted that they learned what worked to move their careers forward through trial-and-error experiences. For many, it was only during our interviews, when asked to reflect back to the key events in their careers, that the career-success principles began to emerge. It was my job to listen for those principles and compare them to the other interviewees' experiences.

My goal in writing this book was to distill what worked in the executives' career successes into principles, guidance and tactics that you can use in your career.

On behalf of all of us who are sharing our career success principles, we have but one wish for you: "Make the most of your talents, education and experience in order to make a positive difference in your work, your community and your personal life. If you do, the rewards of satisfaction, positive relationships and income will follow. Your success will only happen if you are proactive."

Whether you read this book quickly, looking for a basic understanding of the 7 Principles of Career Success, or you use it as a detailed guide for getting your next position, you will clearly be ahead of your competition.

Keep the book nearby as you move around in the organization. At each new level, it will provide insights and tools to adjust your career plan so that you can accelerate your career to arrive at the next-highest level as fast as possible.

CHAPTER 1

Fast Forward Your Career and Take Charge of Your Future at Work: Don't Trust Your Future to Chance or Someone Else

As two Gen X members told me, "Our parents did not take control of their careers as often as maybe they should have. They trusted the organization they worked for to take care of their careers." But for one dad, that didn't work very well. He was laid off twice. Both of these successful Gen X members want to be more proactive in their careers. They do not want to leave their careers to chance. "We'd like to be indispensible," one said, "so that we would be the last people any employer could afford to lose." This wise observation fits in very well with avoiding three common career mistakes.

Common Career Mistakes

Too many ambitious, hard-working and intelligent employees do not get promoted or achieve the career progression as rapidly or as often as they could or should because they make these common mistakes.

1. **They believe that hard work, intelligence and effectiveness will automatically get them promoted.** If employees are not proactively seeking new opportunities, many deserving employ-

ees will be overlooked at promotion time. Why leave your future promotions to chance?

2. **They assume that their boss or the Human Resources Department will make all the right career decisions for them, because the organization always has their best interests in mind.** Your boss and HR may have the best intentions for you, but managing your career is not their job, it is yours.

3. **They do not look for growth opportunities outside their current department.** Limiting your promotion opportunities to replacing your boss when he or she retires or gets promoted can be a huge dead end.

Don't make these mistakes! Instead of relying on hope, luck or someone else for your career success, use the 7 Principles of Career Success to manage your career more successfully. Use these tools to make the most of your career potential.

To help you gain the most from your investment in this book, I have provided:

- A clear statement of what each career-success principle is and how it can work for you, as it has worked for countless others.

- Examples of how each principle worked in various situations.

- Application questions at the end of each chapter. The questions will help you think through the principle and how it applies to you and your career.

- Suggested action steps to help you to apply each principle.

- Tools to help you explore your personal attributes, personality, management and leadership style. These attributes are part of your brand. The more you know about your personality and your work style, the more successfully you can plan and prepare for the future.

- Templates to help you create or refine your career plan, along with planning forms to help you make your career action plan.

Today's Employees Must Take Responsibility for their Career Development

One of the largest consumer products companies, as the result of a merger, had a complete change of management at the top. With the change of management, came a change in how future promotions would occur. Employees could no longer rely on the company to prepare them for future promotion possibilities, as they had done for decades. Employees were now, suddenly responsible for their own future growth.

Instead of management providing the training and development experiences for employees, to prepare them for the next level, they were now advising employees to take charge of their future and anticipate how they should prepare themselves for the next levels in the organization. Future career promotion was no longer automatic. Future opportunities and the qualifications needed to earn them were clearly laid out, but employees now had to compare their current skill sets and experiences against those qualifications. Where they were "short," they needed to take action to become better prepared. This was a monumental shift for the employees.

Today, this philosophy is pretty much the norm in American business. Unlike the '60s and '70s, when many baby boomers began their careers, today there are very few management trainee programs left in even the largest corporations. Formerly such programs hired bright, young employees and then moved them around the company to gain experience in a wide variety of positions and divisions. The programs were expensive. Trainees were not very productive during the years they were in the program. Many either quit or were washed out, resulting in the time invested in them having been lost. Department managers faced a constant influx and outflow of the trainees in their departments.

Today's business environment is much too competitive to carry employees on the payroll who are not yet productive. It is easier to hire qualified people or to point current employees to the next level and require that they acquire the skills needed for the next level, ahead of time. Certainly, companies still invest in training their work forces. But much of that training focuses on specific job skills, safety, and compliance classes; not broad management development programs.

Another change in the workplace is the roll of seniority. Even in some union environments, as well as nonunion jobs, the oldest and longest-serving employee does not automatically get the next promotion. Many companies have set qualification requirements concerning promotions. Seniority, if applicable, applies only to the pool of qualified employees meeting the qualification requirements. So, if only younger employees with low seniority have qualified themselves for the next level, they are the only candidates for promotion.

More Freedom, More Personal Responsibility

Your opportunity for promotion or other career enhancement is limited by job openings in your organization, your qualifications, and the reputation or brand you have established. If you are proactive in preparing yourself for promotion, by adding additional skills and experience (building your brand), you are in a far more likely position to move ahead. You are in an even better spot if you are willing to look for promotion possibilities outside your current department or division.

How ready you are for advancement, however, is now, more than ever, up to you. If you pay attention to the career success principles in this book and apply them, you will be ahead of the vast majority of your peers. Each principle has proven itself by helping others achieve increasingly greater success and satisfaction.

CHAPTER 2

Gender, Generations, and Career Success

Your gender, the generation you were born into and your ethnicity can have an impact on your career success. These same three general characteristics are also present in the employees you work with. You can't change any of the characteristics in yourself, nor can your co-workers change theirs. However, by understanding the characteristics of diverse groups, our organizations and each of us can be more successful.

The face of American business is changing. Already, 15 percent of the millennial or genY generation is in some form of management position. The changing demographics of age, gender and ethnicity will clearly impact your career.

This chapter provides you with an overview of these three demographics. It is meant only as an introduction for you. It precedes the information you need on 7 Principles of Career Success so that you can understand more about the people you will work side-by-side with, and who you may someday manage and lead.

There are more baby boomer men, the majority of them Caucasian, in senior-level positions in organizations of all kinds in America. That fact is neither good nor bad. It is just the way it is for now.

The changing demographics of our culture, however, is already opening up promotion possibilities for women, younger employees from Generation Y (also known as the Millennial Generation) and nonwhite future leaders. Obviously, there will be continuing opportunities for white males.

Baby boomers are beginning to retire in droves. Ten thousand per day turn 65. Boomer retirements will open up a significant number of jobs at all levels in the economy. The future success of American business is not about one age, gender or ethnic group succeeding at the expense of others. More than ever, it is about finding the best people of any background who can bring success to the enterprise.

The overriding message about gender or generations, and career success, is very clear. **"Success is achieved by meeting or exceeding the organization's goals and objectives. It doesn't matter what your gender, education, ethnicity, sexual orientation, or generation is, the goals and objectives must be met."** That is the very direct and uncompromising statement about success criteria from the executives I talked with. However, they also agreed that "how" the objectives are achieved does vary with gender, generation and, to some extent, ethnicity.

Your future success as a leader will depend upon your ability to understand the characteristics of each demographic, especially what drives them. With that knowledge, you can help members of each group make the most of their careers and, therefore, provide the most benefit to the organization you work for.

Gender

Today, more women are executives than ever before. Even though American business has a long way to go toward gender equity (only 17 percent of corporate board positions and 3 percent of board chairs are women), progress is being made.

Maria Bartiromo, anchor of CNBC's *Closing Bell* and anchor and managing editor of *On the Money with Maria Bartiromo*, interviewed the head of the International Monetary Fund, Christine Legarde, in USA Today on April 15, 2013. She asked Legarde, "Why do you think there aren't more female leaders in high places?" She reported to Legarde that Sheryl Sandberg, Facebook COO, had suggested that women do not "lean in." Legarde acknowledged that Sandberg might be right, but "my principle that I have always observed is: Don't imitate the boys. Be yourself and bear the difference. It has to do with having sufficient confidence in yourself and having confidence in others so that you can actually afford to be different, and be proud of it. And enrich by demonstrating diversity."

The female executives I interviewed felt strongly that in the future there will be more women in executive positions, because the support systems, role models, and education systems will enable more women to make career choices that lead to executive positions.

Let's look at the experiences many of today's successful women executives faced in their careers. Those who began their careers in the '60s and '70s faced sexual harassment, pressure from their parents to seek only the "acceptable" careers: teacher, nurse, secretary and, eventually, homemaker. If you watch the TV series "Mad Men," you get some sense of what women faced in that era.

Women began working outside their homes in large numbers during World War II. Millions of men were in uniform, fighting in Europe and in the South Pacific. Women worked in defense plants, making bullets, bombs, airplanes, and more. Did you know that most were fired when the men came home from the war? While some women got a taste of the economic independence that came from having their own income and stayed in the workforce when they could, most returned to "domestic" life.

If a woman did seek a business career in the '50s, '60s and '70s, she had to wear dark blue suits, low heels, short hair, and little or no makeup or jewelry. Above all, a woman was expected to respect male leadership. After all, men were the "bread winners" for their families. Women who advanced tended to work in retail, human resources, marketing, communications, accounting, finance, and in customer service departments. Few worked in skilled trades as electricians, engineers, plumbers, linemen, or truck drivers. Very few were supervisors, managers or corporate officers.

Few were in charge of engineering or field operations. If they did manage others, it was typically other women.

Today's female executive is generally free of most, but not all, of the barriers and stigmas her predecessors faced. Women today have more female role models and female mentors, but business leaders are still predominately male. Depending upon the organization and the industry it functions in, a woman may still have to pay close attention to her relationships with male colleagues.

Most of the female executives I interviewed said there were two significant influences that helped them achieve their success.

First, they generally credited their parents, especially their fathers, with having given them the encouragement to become whatever they chose. There were inspiring tales of parents and siblings supporting unconventional educational and work experiences. In effect, they felt free to choose any career that appealed to them, and they felt supported in their choice. That was not the case for most of their mothers and aunts a generation earlier. But even today, only 18 percent of women, compared to 36 percent of men, aspire to be top executives, according to a 2012 McKinsey study.

Second, most of the women executives benefited from a strong male mentor or two who recognized their talents and either gave them the opportunity to express them, or even pushed them into challenging situations where they could shine.

"Women bring different skills into the mix," observed one female executive. "Women tend to have strong emotional IQs, and they are multi-taskers. Women tend to be more open. Certainly, there are men who also have these traits, but in general, women exhibit them more."

Every female executive reiterated that "both men and women must deliver results, make things happen, and improve the bottom line. There is no gender difference when it comes to results."

"The difference comes in how we achieve the results. There is no one way to make things work successfully," explained another female executive. "Everyone brings unique perspectives, talents and skills to work. The best organizations make the most of that divergence and leverage it for greater success."

"We are seeing a change in the number of women in our industry who hold field or technical positions," observed a male COO, "I can only imagine how tough it must be for some of them, given that they are often the only female on a crew, or they are one of the few female crew leaders. Men have had the benefit of a network that has developed over the years."

In the utility industry, the Midwest Energy Association's Energetic Women initiative is a great resource for women to build their connections and for men to better appreciate the special challenges women face. The key for any employee, male or female, is to have support resources to help them deliver the highest level of performance on behalf of customers and the organization. In the end, it is performance that counts."

"Thank heavens, women are now able to be female in the workplace," said another female executive. "We are often mothers, spouses, partners, and community volunteers, as well as organizational leaders. We are not trying to be clones of our male counterparts. We love to compete and celebrate the contribution we, and our teams, make to the organization's overall success. I don't see my career as a female competing with males, but rather, I see collaboration, where the best of each gender helps the organization move forward. Today's most effective leaders appreciate what each gender brings to the workplace."

"Women are needed in so many areas," said an employment expert, "especially in engineering, math and science fields. There are great opportunities for recent grads in these fields. Later, with those initial credentials, promotions to management and leadership, roles can come quickly. The more women can improve their performance through networking and being mentored, as well as mentoring others, the more effective women can be at work."

I don't want to give female readers, especially those who are just beginning their careers, an unrealistic view of the challenges they face at work. Clearly, the multiple roles of a female executive, spouse, mother, family organizer, etc., are difficult to balance. My intent is not to answer the question, "Can a woman have it all?" There are hundreds of books on that subject. I will say only that these are issues that women, and increasingly men, need to face as they move forward in their careers. Ignoring them isn't smart if you want to take charge of your future at work.

One woman colleague of mine handled the "have it all" question this way. While making polite conversation during a break in a meeting we were attending, I asked her what she and her family were doing for July 4th. She said, "I have no idea. My husband takes care of planning our family activities." I was surprised, and apparently she sensed my reaction. She immediately explained, "My husband and I sat down early in our marriage, when our careers were just being launched. We agreed that we wanted to have a family someday, but we did not want our children to be raised by others in a day-care situation. So, we very honestly discussed both of our careers and the potential earnings and overall success both of us might achieve. We also discussed what we wanted from our careers and our family life. Ultimately, we decided that my husband would handle the day-to-day raising of our family when the time came. That decision allowed me the freedom to go 'all out' in my career. I have a great relationship with my husband and my children, and they are proud of their father and of me."

Clearly, not every family will make this choice, but for this family it has worked out beautifully. Each family or set of partners needs to discuss the issue of career growth and the impact that it will have on the primary relationship, as well as on family and friends.

Generations

"Generational differences are real," explained a COO, "and understanding how each generational group looks at work and life should be an important consideration within every organization. Real effectiveness comes when supervisors, managers, and officers learn how to take the best traits of each generation and mold them into an even more powerful organization."

Leaders who can leverage generational differences—in terms of how each group processes information, uses technology, views work-life balance, and experiences the world at large—can better tap into each person's gifts, energy, and passion to achieve greater levels of success.

Generations of the Past and Those at Work Today

The **Greatest Generation** was born between 1900 and 1925. The vast majority retired many years ago, and many have passed on. These are the folks who lived through World War I, the Great Depression and World War II. They experienced shortages of food, housing, and transportation in a very direct way, which most workers today never have. They knew sacrifice in a deep and personal way. For them, there was no use complaining, because almost everyone in America was experiencing the same thing.

The **Silent Generation** (also known as Traditionalists) was born between 1926 and 1945. They also experienced WWII, the Korean War, and, those born early in the group, the Depression. This is the generation that after WWII saw the dramatic growth of America into a world power. Hard work and education were the keystones of a better life. They felt a tremendous sense that anything was possible. The future was bright, and they had learned how to work. Some women in this generation had "tasted" the freedom of full-time work outside the home in defense jobs until the servicemen came home. This is a generation that tends not to look back and talk about their early life, especially the hardships.

Baby Boomers were born between 1946 and 1964. They are the children of the post-WWII families who also grew up believing that anything was possible. Their innocence and reality were dramatically changed when they experienced the assassinations of President John F. Kennedy, Martin Luther King, Jr., and Robert Kennedy. They also saw the ravages of the Vietnam War, the civil rights movement, and the women's movement on their televisions every night. They grew up learning how to take shelter from nuclear bombs, by hiding under their desks at school. Even though some boomers rebelled against societal norms and corporate life in their youth; most settled down into suburban life and 9-to-5 work routines.

Generation X members were born between 1965 and 1980. Unlike the boomers, whose families in the 1950s and early '60s often had stay-at-home moms, both parents of Gen Xers typically worked outside the home. In order to have the American Dream: a house in the suburbs, two cars, vacations at Disneyland, and Nike tennis shoes, many in this generation were raised in nursery schools or were "latch-key" kids, coming home to an empty house after school. This group is much less individualistic, and they are, therefore, more collaborative. It's the way they grew up. Their boomer parents tended to provide their gen X children with more luxuries at earlier ages, without expecting them to "earn" them, as their parents had.

Millennials or Generation Y members were born between 1981 and, roughly, 2002. This group grew up with digital toys, computers and cell phones, and is very comfortable in researching and gathering information on the Internet. They may have hundreds of

"Facebook Friends," but many lack interpersonal skills, according to research with college freshmen. Even in a face-to-face meeting around a conference table, a group of millennials may all have their laptops open and be collaborating with each other on them. They are sometimes called the "digital tribe."

The reason I raise the issue of generations and careers is two-fold.

First, while there are always exceptions to any generalization, there are generalized traits that are common to each generation. Those traits must be understood by all aspiring leaders from each generation because, as our workplace diversifies with a greater mix of generations, different generations will be working with and for each other more than ever. As you will see later in the book, understanding yourself, your personality, work style, etc., is an important part of being ready for career advancement. Part of who you are may be a function of your generational traits. As you understand the traits of your own generation, you can determine to what extent you exhibit those traits, good and not so good.

Second, rather than being critical of each generation's negative traits (each generation has them), leaders should understand how to focus on the positive traits and engage each group in the future success of the enterprise. It is too easy to "blow off" the generations you are not part of and assume their traits are the problem, and that they don't understand your generation.

Here's an example of very diverse points of view based on different life experiences between Baby Boomers and Millennials. Boomers generally feel they grew to maturity earlier and that they were not "over protected" by their parents. A colleague of mine was born in 1946 and received a suitcase from her family on her 18th birthday. Her older brothers and sisters had already received their suitcases. Mom and dad wished her well and invited her back for Sunday dinner, but she was expected to take charge of her life at 18. She had to find a job, find a place to live, and get on with her life.

On the other hand, the Millennial Generation members are not becoming responsible for their lives as early in any similar way. In 2007-2009, according to Zhenchao Qian of Ohio State University and the US 2010 Project, 43 percent of young people aged 20 to 24 were living at home in 2012, as were 19 percent of those 25 to 29 and 9 percent of those 30 to 34. What a different set of life experiences the early boomer had when she left home at 18, as compared to those still living at home today, as indicated by the study. What kind of work ethic and expectations would an 18-year-old have when receiving no support from home, versus a 30-year-old who still lives at home? The ironic thing is that some of those boomers who left home at 18, 19 or during their early 20s are now the parents of the 20 to 30-year-old "somethings" still living at home. There may be very practical reasons for still living at home today, but the life experiences are different than those of Boomers.

"Wanted: Millennials Who Know How to Interview" was the headline in the B section of USA Today on April 30, 2013. Paul Davidson's article subtitle was "Clueless grads fail job interviews by texting, taking calls." The article included stories of parents interacting with employers, of taking pets to job interviews, a sense of entitlement and more.

In a Beyond.com study of 6,361 job seekers and veteran Human Resource Professionals conducted in April and May of 2013 and quoted in the June 10, 2013, Money section of USA Today, the following differences in perception were rather extreme. Sixty-five percent of Millennials described themselves as "people-savvy," as compared to only 14 percent of the HR professionals. Only 11 percent of the HR professionals describe Millennials as hard-working. But 86 percent of the millenials described themselves as hard-working. Those are just two examples of the rather large divide in perceptions.

I am not being critical of all Millennials nor all Boomers. It is the difference in perspective between generations that I want you to understand, because these perspectives show up at work.

Here's another Boomer vs. Gen X/Millennial comparison. As a boomer child myself, I was free to wander my neighborhood as young as five. I walked to kindergarten in Minnesota, winters and all, four blocks away. We had few toys, and television was a big black box in the corner, reserved for Sunday nights. We played board and outdoor games, created our own clubs, and built forts in the nearby woods. As the neighborhood kids and I reached the middle grades of elementary school, and into middle school, our after-school activities were provided by the school, at the school. From the 5th grade on, I played on two different school basketball teams, and a third was sponsored by my church. The school activity bus took me home at 6 p.m. each day. My parents supported me by attending my games, but they were spectators, not coaches or league organizers like many parents are today. My nights and weekends were not "managed" for me, with tons of activities. A "play date" did not exist for me, unless I arranged something myself with my friends, usually outside.

Younger parents reading this are probably shocked. Wandering the neighborhood at five! Playing outdoor games in the dark somewhere in the neighborhood when in grade school! Spending whole summer days hiking, and cooking lunch in the woods, when only 10 or 11! Many '50s moms were at home all day and they looked out for all the children in the neighborhood. Clearly, growing up in the '50s and early '60s was a different experience than growing up today.

Boomers are often criticized by younger generations for "living to work" and Xers and Millennials are criticized for only wanting to "work to live." It is common for younger generation members to refuse to work overtime. Boomers, especially those born in the late '40s and early '50s, may have fought for civil rights, protested the Vietnam War, and marched for equal rights for women, but they quickly became compliant employees when they married and became homeowners and parents. Boomers are accustomed to an annual performance review and, hopefully, a merit pay increase, and a cost of living adjustment. Working overtime was a plus for most boomer workers. It was a boost to family income.

Xers and Millennials were raised with a different kind of parental involvement. If a boomer was not doing well in school, it was the boomer's fault, and the answer was to study harder. Today, parents tend to blame the school, teachers or other authority figures if their child is not doing well. Today's parents tend to organize their children's lives much more completely. Weekends and evenings are often devoted to driving their children to dance, swimming, soccer, and other kinds of lessons and events. Boomer parents were there for their children, too, but there was much more free time for kids to create their own activities.

The parenting psychology today is often "no child ever fails. Even if we lost the game, we should hold our heads high." For some, this created a world where Xers and Millennials never learned from their mistakes or losses, because they never experienced failure. This resulted in either a sense of arrogance or they grew up afraid of failure (risk averse) and in need of almost constant positive reinforcement. An HR director, herself a Gen X member, told me that for some millennial team members, her company has modified its performance review procedure. Now the company sends a written performance review to the individual first. This allows the employee to process any negative feedback and discuss it with parents or friends. Only after this processing time is the employee asked to come in and sit down with their boss for a one-on-one. Boomers might scoff at such a system, but the HR director says it works. Everyone gets the same scheduled review and is held to the same standard. The organization has simply adjusted its procedures to be certain a significant and growing generation of employee leaders gets the performance reviews they need in a process that works for them.

A personal growth coach offered the following: "There is no clear pattern that I see with younger people so far. I have had young clients on both ends of the spectrum. I have a college student client who already has her own business. She is so committed to her personal growth that she pays for coaching out of her own pocket. She is amazing. I also had a client who was the epitome of what the media tells us is wrong with the Millennial Generation. This young man, whom I was to help learn how to interview more successfully, exhibited poor posture, offered no eye contact, had a hard time putting a sentence together, and was poorly dressed. He was obviously not motivated personally and came to see me because someone else was paying for it."

Recent research indicates that nationally, Gen Y workers don't tend to have jobs inside the largest U.S. companies. The highest concentration of Millennials, 47 percent, work for companies with fewer than 100 employees; followed by medium-sized companies that have between 100 and 1,500 employees (30 percent). The fewest, 23 percent, work in companies with more than 1,500 employees.

As I said before, leaders shouldn't judge one generation's experiences and traits against another. Rather, we should seek to understand that, as a general rule, each generation was raised differently and is likely to bring different traits to work. Understanding the differences between employees is smart business and smart leadership. A successful leader must understand all team members: what motivates them, how they learn best, what they have in common, and how to make the most of the collective talents of the team.

> **But remember, regardless of your generation, or your gender, performance expectations and goals do not change.**

A computer software CEO told me, "When I am looking for good people, I'll take motivated, loyal, assertive, curious people of any generation. I want employees who are not afraid to work at the job. I'll hire employees with these credentials over candidates with top 1 percent career pedigrees if the pedigreed applicants have an entitlement attitude or are lacking those other traits."

Lessons for today's leaders: what are Gen Xers looking for in their work?

In my monthly interviews, I met a broad range of Gen X employees who were on their way up, as well as Gen X senior executives who were already there. One interview in particular, with two 30ish Gen Xers, a husband and wife, seemed to sum up the inputs of many younger interviewees.

I asked the couple about their career satisfactions thus far and what they believed would keep them engaged in their work in the future. The wife works as an event planner for a private club. Her duties also include marketing and event sales. The husband was recently promoted to the position of area sales manager for a major manufacturer of residential building products. Previously, he was a manufacturing supervisor and most recently a salesman for the same company, so he really knows the product he sells.

Both partners, liberal arts college grads, listed their satisfactions:

1. Doing good work for their clients and their employer by melding the needs together for mutual satisfaction.

2. Being independent: "My organization trusts me and backs me up on the decisions I make."

3. Learning new things. Being able to learn more about the total company, sales, operations, and customer relations is a special part of their work satisfaction.

4. Winning. Making sales and solving problems to delight clients.

5. Being open and direct with their bosses. "The more direct we can be, the less chance for misunderstandings and greater success all around."

6. Having a positive impact on the organization.

7. Being held to high standards. Neither spouse wants to work for an organization that accepts mediocre performance from them, or

from anyone else.

So, what have these two individuals discovered thus far that does not work for them?

1. Working for a boss who makes promises, but does not deliver on them.

2. Not being recognized and compensated for consistently superior performance. Under those conditions, gen Xers are less likely than boomers to hang around.

3. Lacking growth opportunity.

Different Work Styles Still Achieve High Performance

"To compete, organizations will have to make decisions faster. We have access to more information and data today than ever before. Customer expectations are considerably higher and there will be a great deal more new technology," offered a boomer senior executive. "Organizations will have to be more comfortable with the use of technology. That's where gen X and the even younger millennial generation professionals will be a huge boost for us. As long as we are careful not to let technology separate us from each other, this wave of younger employees will lead the way for us because they have grown up with technology all around them. We are already learning that younger workers have different lifestyle habits. Some do not want overtime. Young families want flexibility to balance life when both spouses work hard. These new perspectives and the hard-working people who have them will blend with the older, more traditional workforce. That is inevitable. We need to appreciate the best of both. Together, we will have to be willing to take risks in order to achieve outstanding results."

During the interview with the gen X couple, I asked if they had heard the criticism some boomers have expressed about younger people not working as hard as employees from older generations. Yes, they had heard the comment and both agreed that, like any generational group, there are some of their peers who don't have the drive to succeed.

However, they said, <u>there is a fundamental difference in the way their generation works, as compared to their parents.</u> "Our parents segmented their lives. Work was separate from family or personal time. "To us," said the pair, "we work just as hard, but in our own way. We don't segment our day. We mix things together. Work, social connections and interests are part of our whole day. We are just as likely to be on our iPads and laptops in the evening, doing work, as we might spend some time during the day checking in on our interests online. <u>It is a different work-life style, but we are just as driven by a need to succeed and to do good work.</u>"

Take a moment and reflect on your own generation. What are its characteristics? What motivates your peers? How is your generation different from older and younger generations? How might those differences play out in your career progression? How does an appreciation for the strengths of each generation at work help you make a more positive contribution in your current and future positions?

Whatever gender, ethnic or generational differences may exist at work, the goals and objectives of our employers must still be met. Employers expect everyone to do their part to achieve organization-wide success. The "how" each diverse person or group achieves results may vary based upon our unique backgrounds, but the "what" we need to do for our employer doesn't change.

Your ethnicity may bring with it certain cultural values that might be different from those of your peers at work. Some cultures are more assertive, others more passive. Some have different attitudes toward gender, and even toward age groups. Personal habits may be different.

As an employee, it pays to be aware of how the corporate or work team culture relates to your personal habits and values.

As a successful leader, just as with gender and generation differences, it is important to blend the best of any group of employees into a winning combination. Your ability to honor differences within your team is a significant leadership trait.

CHAPTER 3

Understand the 7 Principles of Career Success, Level 1

There are seven key principles that are important for you to understand and use, in order to make the most of your career. Individually, each principle is helpful, but collectively they are very powerful.

In this book, I have dedicated a chapter to each of the seven principles. The narrative explains each principle in more detail and offers examples of how each principle helped move forward the 60 plus successful executive interviewees' careers.

The 7 principles are divided into two sections, Level 1 and Level 2. The first three principles, **Get Connected and Get Noticed, Be a Star Where You Are**, and **Know Yourself and Want You Want,** are especially critical in the very earliest stages of your career. Think about it. If the decision makers in your organization do not know who you are, or you are not really being fully successful today in your current job, your career success is very limited. And, if you do not know what you want from your career and do not have a good understanding of your own personality and work traits, you may end up pursuing a career path that is not going to be effective or satisfying. The chapters about each principle will give you very specific tools to help you improve your visibility within your organization, understand what it takes to be a star in your current position, and what the best future direction is for you at each stage of your career.

As you move higher in the organization, the first three principles continue to be important. You will apply them in different ways at each new level you achieve. The higher you rise, the larger your network, the broader your "star" contribution needs to be and the more you will want to understand your leadership and thinking styles as you plan your next career move.

In Level 2, the last four principles are covered, beginning in chapter 7. Here is an overview of all 7 principles.

The 7 Principles of Career Success

Level 1: Establish Your Brand
- Get Connected & Get Noticed
- Be a Star Where You Are
- Know Yourself & What You Want

Level 2: Build Your Brand
- Understand the Business
- Be Ready
- Grow as a Leader
- Never Say Never

Make Your Plan and Work It: Update Regularly

Level 1

1. Get Connected and Get Noticed. No one gets ahead without help. Learn how to make the connections that will help you at every level of your career. Learn how to get noticed so you are always in the promotion pool. A section on mentors and mentoring is included, with even more information available on mentoring in Appendix A.

2. Be a Star Where You Are. Your future success begins with strong performance in your current job. Learn how to be even more effective in the job posting you are now in. Learn about the "extras" that mark you as exceptional.

3: Know Yourself and What You Want. How well do you know yourself? What is your management style? What is your motivation to move your career forward? What are your personality traits? Knowing the answers to these questions means you have taken an inventory of your current strengths and "needs-improvement" areas. This is a significant career success principle, because only with these insights can you grow and make the best possible career choices.

Level 2

4. Understand the Big Picture. The more you know about your organization and your industry—how it operates, who it serves, its finances, and its future challenges—the stronger your future will be. Whether you want to be promoted or move into that special new job assignment you really want, you are a more valuable employee if you know more than just how your own department works. The more you know about the overall organization and your industry, the better your "brand" is in your organization.

5. Be Ready. Develop yourself and be ready for promotion before the next job opening occurs. If a great job opens up, but you are missing key skills or experience, few organizations can afford to wait for you to catch up. Learn what the requirements are for the next job you want and fill any gaps you may now have. Your competition may already have the needed skills and experience for the new opening.

6. Grow Your Leadership Skills. Organizations are ultimately about people. Even the most reclusive, highly technical employee must interact with fellow employees. The more successful you are, the more people will look up to you. Respect is one of the characteristics of a leader. Leaders are made, not born. You can learn to be a stronger leader at every level of your career.

7. Never Say Never. Get out of your comfort zone. Be willing to take on new challenges and take some calculated risks. Learn to look for and benefit from "Butterfly" moments (those scary situations that, when overcome, are real career boosters).

Application Tools: Make a Career Plan and Make It Work

What do you want to accomplish in your career? Do you want to be a specialist (individual contributor), a manager, or a senior executive? With your career plan in place, starting with where you are today, you can build a plan so that your future success is in your hands, not someone else's. A checklist and planning forms are provided in this chapter.

Your career will span 30, 40, maybe 50 years. Applying the 7 Principles of Career Success will help ensure that you get the career satisfaction you want, whether that means being promoted, regularly, ahead of your peers, or landing that special position that is truly fulfilling.

Ultimately, career success depends upon a variety of factors, but you now have a head start because you know about the 7 Principles of Career Success in this book. Use this power to your advantage.

Obviously you can't control every aspect of your career. The economy, mergers, the sale of your company, or personnel changes at the top of your organization are events over which you have no control. These factors can affect your career from time to time, but the regular application, by you, of the 7 Principles of Career Success is still your best insurance for long-term career success.

Remember, successful people control as much of their future at work as they can. They don't trust their career to chance or assume that their boss or HR will take care of their careers.

CHAPTER 4

Career Success Principle Number 1: Get Connected & Get Noticed: No One Gets Ahead Without Help

Fast Forward ⏩ Your Career

Level 1: Establish Your Brand
- **Get Connected & Get Noticed**
- Be a Star Where You Are
- Know Yourself & What You Want

Level 2: Build Your Brand
- Understand the Business
- Be Ready
- Grow as a Leader
- Never Say Never

Make Your Plan and Work It: Update Regularly

Here's One Way to Get Noticed.

Bob was one of the youngest employees ever invited to speak from the head table. All of the other speakers were much more experienced and had job titles well above his. But the chairman felt that Bob had an important message to share at the annual conference in Las Vegas.

Bob got a standing ovation from the entire crowd of over 1,200 employees and the executive team, even before he started his speech. Here's how:

All the speakers and the other executives at the head table had wireless microphones attached to their lapels so that they could answer questions if called upon without passing a microphone around.

Bob was quite nervous about his presentation. He knew that it was a big opportunity. After finishing his dinner, Bob sat at the head table, waiting for the introductions and the first presentations to begin. It didn't take long for him to realize that something he ate had not agreed with him, and he felt the need to slip out and make a trip to the restroom. He quietly left the head table, went to the restroom and then returned to the main dining room. When he entered the room, much to his surprise, he received a standing round of applause from everyone in the room. Regrettably, Bob had left his wireless microphone on while in the restroom. Every bathroom sound had been captured and broadcast over the hotel's speaker system to the entire ballroom and all the guests.

Clearly, that was not how Bob wanted to be "noticed." Though embarrassing at the time, he received a second standing ovation for his presentation, and went on to a very successful career. He would be the first to suggest that there are much better ways to get positively "noticed" within your organization.

Remember that, regardless of which broad career path you are on, becoming the highest level career specialist/technical person (sometimes called individual contributor) in your department, or moving into the management/leadership track, successful organizations are ultimately about people relationships. Those relationships are with the organization's stakeholders: employees, customers, investors, government officials and the community at large. It should not be a surprise, then, to learn from successful executives that being able to establish good relationships is a big part of their career success.

Naturally, your closest relationships are with co-workers and your boss. They are the people with whom you spend the most time, and they are the people who know you best.

Obviously, positive relationships with the people you work most closely with provide the first step in getting noticed in a positive way. Poor relationships within our own department mean you are not likely to be in the promotion pool until you improve them.

On the other hand, great relationships with co-workers and your boss, don't guarantee your success, either, because many organizations have adopted organization-wide Succession Planning Systems (SPS). These systems attempt to capture "high potential" candidates from throughout the company, so that a broader base of future management talent can be identified and developed. The use of these systems typically means that your department, or division manager, has to consider candidates from other areas of the company when filling a vacancy in your department. Your competitors could be anywhere in the company.

This may be bad news for you, if you are the in-the-department "star" who is not well known outside your department. You might be passed over in favor of a broader array of more broadly known candidates who are already part of the company-wide succession planning pool. The good news is that if you can increase your visibility across the organization, you could be a candidate for many more promotional opportunities in other departments or divisions.

Department Rock Star Is Sidelined

Rick started as a marketing assistant after completing college and a short stint working for a state agency in PR. His boss was an officer in the same United States Army Reserve unit that Rick was in. Rick's boss believed he had the potential to make a real contribution in the marketing department, where the boss was a senior manager in charge of promotion.

After a few years of promotions into new assignments every six to nine months, Rick's progression stopped.

"I don't understand what happened," Rick confided to a college friend. "It seemed that everyone liked my work. My boss has been promoting me ahead of everyone. In fact, some of those folks, even though they have been with the company for many years, now report to me. My boss's boss, the VP of marketing, is always cordial and seems to celebrate the progress my team and I are making in several areas. I feel that he has me in his sights for the future. But now, it seems that I am stuck and I don't know why."

Rick had two problems that he wasn't aware of.

First, his rapid rise in a normally conservative company made some people in other departments nervous because he was virtually unknown outside marketing. Although Rick was friendly and committed to the company's success, not just his own, he had not participated in any broader company activities and he did not have any kind of a network outside the marketing department. Overall, the company was focused on operations and finance, so just being a star in marketing didn't help Rick in the company at large. He needed to become better known, not only by his peers, but by other department heads and officers so that they would welcome him into the promotion pool of "high potential" employees.

Rick's second problem was that his boss had become concerned that Rick might be promoted out of Marketing. That would mean that his boss would have to take on Rick's work until he could find another Rick. The boss was a very creative guy, but he was frustrated that his own career seemed to be stuck one notch below VP. The situation had become so bad, that when the division VP asked Rick's boss about promoting Rick to a higher position outside Marketing, Rick's boss said he knew Rick would not be interested. Consequently, the opportunity was never offered to Rick.

Rick discovered this last problem when he spoke with the VP in the cafeteria. After some polite conversation, the VP said, "Rick, I am surprised that you are not interested in the job over in Customer Relations. I thought that would be a great next step for you."

Rick's face betrayed his surprise and the VP noticed.

"Well," Rick said, "I am sorry you got that impression. Actually, I would be very interested in the move. I love what I am doing, and Tom has been really good to me from the beginning, but I can see that we have a great opportunity to upgrade our customer satisfaction numbers if we can solve some challenges in Customer Service. I'd love to be able to make a contribution there."

The VP sighed in frustration, realizing that Tom, Rick's boss, had misled him about Rick's interest in the new assignment.

Rick's Way Forward

Rick didn't realize it at the time, but he could have avoided these problems by expanding his internal and external networks. If he had confided in peers elsewhere in his division that he was interested in challenges outside his immediate area of expertise, they might have helped the division VP understand Rick's interests. Rick also got too comfortable having his boss push him forward in the division. He did not realize then that depending upon just one person to take care of his career was not a good long-term strategy. He also needed to build relationships outside his division, to build trust and confidence.

So, how do you become one of those "high potential" candidates who the succession planning system seems to provide with more opportunities for promotion? Performance and potential are vital, of course, but to get into the company-wide promotion pool means that a broad group of senior management needs to know about you. If they do not know you and your work, they can't actively work to see that you get more opportunities to move ahead.

Do the Right People Out There Know You Exist?

"I get by with a little help from my friends," is not only a line from a famous Beatles' song, but it also sums up the career success observations of many of the executives I talked with.

Top 10 Ways to Get Connected and Get Noticed

It can be difficult to get experience and recognition in different areas of the company, especially when your career is fairly new. Here are 10 proven ways:

1. Task forces and committee work. Find one and volunteer.
   Suzanne's specialty was research and numbers, but she lacked operating experience and was often kidded about being a numbers "nerd." She felt she had the potential to manage people, but at the moment she was not optimistic about getting the chance.

   She heard about a continuous improvement initiative in the operating division. From what she read about the project, she felt that her current expertise would be an asset and that she could learn a great deal about how operations really worked. After consultation with her boss, she approached the head of the project and volunteered. The team clearly needed her technical skills, and she was selected.

   After two years of difficult work, the team not only received approval of some significant changes in the way in which the organization delivered its services, but Suzanne had built several significant relationships in other areas of the company. Her work with field personnel during the research and testing phases of the project brought her to the attention of several operations managers. There was no automatic promotion into management, but her work definitely enhanced her professional brand. It took a year, but she was promoted into a manager's position.

2. Take a lateral move and transfer into another department.

This can be a very smart tactic. Just having the courage to take the chance is enough to get noticed sometimes. The fact that you are learning another part of the business and performing well in a new position is even more impressive. With a lateral move (or a promotion into a new area), you now have experience in more than one area. The broader your experience, the more likely that you will be considered for moves, including promotions, into other divisions. Too many people limit themselves by staying in their comfort zones within just one department or division.

3. Build relationships with peers in other parts of the organization.

Solid relationships throughout the organization provide you with learning opportunities, and you are more likely to get the help and support you may need in the future.

One savvy manager decided that, after a 3-way merger, she would contact her counterparts in the other two companies, now divisions, of the much larger combined organization. Initially, she encountered some skepticism concerning her efforts to share information. Each of the other peer managers assumed they were in competition with each other and that they should be loyal only to their previous division managements. But, over a period of several months, all three managers began to benefit from discussions about how each approached various work situations. When a natural disaster struck in the home area of one of the divisions, the other two were able to send assistance quickly because they understood how that division operated. The reputations of all three managers were enhanced by their ability to handle the crisis more effectively than most others.

Another senior director made a point to build a network across his company. "I always established and maintained relationships with six to eight operating leaders in other areas of the company. They knew me on a personal level, and we understood each other's challenges. However, e-mails and telephone calls alone did not build the depth of relationship I felt we needed. I made certain we spent some face time. With that deeper connection, it was easier to have difficult conversations or to respond to requests for help that required some sacrifices. Those types of situations were much less stressful because, while we were not fast friends, we knew each other and there was a basis of trust."

4. Find one or more mentors in other parts of the company.

They can help you with more than honest feedback and advice. They can help you understand what their division does and how all the divisions work together to make the company a success.

Clarissa worked closely with several senior officers as an internal HR consultant while the company was instituting a new pay-for-performance system. Through the give and take with one officer, she built a relationship of mutual respect. Within a year, that officer was promoted, and then headed a business unit. Although their professional relationship was now fairly distant, as Clarissa's work was done for the company on the pay system, the new division head called Clarissa. He said, "I have a job in operations that I think you could perform successfully. It is totally outside your technical expertise, but you will have technical staff to help you with that. I need fresh eyes and new perspectives, and you have demonstrated the ability to bring out the best in people in a short time. I have confidence that you can handle this."

A number of the executives who contributed to the book had similar experiences. Ultimately, the organization is looking for performers who can "connect the dots" by seeing patterns others see only as individual pieces of information. Being able to see the patterns, formulate a plan, execute it with inspired team members, and then live with the results is a powerful resumé-building tool, no matter what company you work for. Good mentors can help you develop such skills, and then help you find opportunities where you can use them.

5. Hang Out With Successful People.

"If you are going to hang out with people in your organization anyway, why not hang out with the successful ones," quipped a Chief Operating Officer (COO). "I learned a lot about other parts of the company as I was making my way up the chain of command. I found that successful people have attitudes that are positive and infectious." He went on to suggest that those individuals who are leaders today, or who are likely to be tomorrow, are great resources for learning success principles. If more and more successful people in the organization know you and what your interests and capabilities are, you will have an even stronger network of people who can support your career.

This COO was not suggesting that successful people should only hang out with the high-level superstars. As an effective leader, he also makes a special effort to listen and talk with people at all levels in his organization. He knows that spending time with the "doers" at all levels is very important in building a base of folks who will have your back when needed. Recognizing the contributions of those you work with, from front line positions such as administrative assistants, order entry people, customer service representatives, etc., honors their contribution to the organization and, through your positive relationship with them, you learn what is really going on in the business.

6. Trust Your People: They Will Enhance Your Brand.

A former nuclear submarine officer who rose to command more than 8,000 U.S. Navy sailors, and now has a senior-level position in civilian manufacturing, made the same point in an interview. "If you want people to 'have your back' when you need support most, then you have to demonstrate that you trust their professionalism by listening to their advice and letting them do their jobs. I learned quickly to listen to the people who knew their jobs better than I ever could. My job was to clear the way for them to succeed. As a result, I succeeded."

7. Participate in Charitable or Other Volunteer Activities.

Successful organizations encourage "good citizenship" by sponsoring community activities. They also encourage employees to participate. Volunteering in service to community organizations can be a very useful career building tactic, and it's also the right thing to do.

Two CEOs were having lunch after a round of golf at a charity golf outing. They knew each other because they were both on the board of the charity that served their community well. Harold was impressed with the volunteers Scott's company supplied to plan the golf event. "Scott, I was really impressed with Robb Alvarez," Harold said, "He is really a great idea guy and he gets people fired up. The golf tournament hole sponsorships and the silent auction brought in a lot more money than last year, thanks to his chairing the fundraising committee. How long has Alvarez been with your organization?" Ironically, Scott wasn't sure because Scott had never had occasion to work directly with Alvarez. Alvarez wasn't on Scott's radar. Harold's positive comments piqued Scott's interest, however, and he put Alvarez on his watch list.

Alvarez did not take on the fundraising task for the charity event as a specific career enhancer, but the result was very positive for him. Sometimes community service work can raise your reputation within your current employer's organization. It can also bring you to the attention of other employers in the community. In Alvarez's situation, he could probably get an interview with Harold's company if he wanted it.

Contributing your time and talent to a community organization can be doubly rewarding. It offers both a sense of personal satisfaction from helping a worthwhile organization and it can clearly enhance your reputation and build your brand.

Even if your CEO does not receive a direct compliment about you, as Alvarez's CEO did, community organizations generally send thank-you letters to company officers recognizing employee volunteer service.

Another benefit of community volunteer experience is learning from others who work for other organizations. Sometimes, observing leaders with different backgrounds can be a great source of personal growth.

Every successful executive I interviewed mentioned the value of volunteering with organizations such as Boy or Girl Scouts, Habitat for Humanity, Big Brother/Big Sisters, food banks, United Way, and hundreds of other organizations. They recognized that these organizations need motivated and hard–working volunteers.

8. Build Great Connections Outside Your Organization.

Rotary, Lions, Sertoma, Toastmaster's, and local professional groups in your interest area (accounting, HR, IT, etc.) can provide significant professional contacts and career connections. Making a point of meeting people and maintaining contact with them is another important tactic.

Harvey MacKay is a businessman, professional speaker and nationally published columnist. MacKay is also well known as the author of five business bestsellers, including *Swim With the Sharks, Beware the Naked Man Who Offers You His Shirt* and *Dig Your Well Before You're Thirsty*. He earns more than $50,000 for every keynote speech he gives.

I first met MacKay when he was a commercial envelope salesman. I was the envelope buyer for the local utility in MacKay's home town. I bought 3,000,000 envelopes a year from him. Some years later, MacKay was hired by a mentor of mine to consult on a project, and we connected again. Five years after that, MacKay was an even more successful author and public speaker. We found ourselves seated next to each other on an airplane. He remembered our previous meetings, and we chatted amiably about where our careers had taken each of us. A week later, I received a "care package" from MacKay. He sent me personally autographed copies of every one of his books and a brand new audio series he had just completed on *How to Build a Network of Power Relationships*. Even though he had become an even-more successful author, national columnist, and an in-demand convention speaker, he was still striving to be better known. The books and the audio series he sent to me are still in my library.

9. Industry Trade Associations Provide Connections and Successful Practices.

Participation in industry trade associations is another way to build relationships, add new skills, and build your brand. Almost every industry has a national, regional and/or state trade association. Trade associations are membership organizations that have companies or other organizations as members. Virtually every industry has at least one. Most associations monitor federal and state legislation and regulations. They often lobby with legislators and regulators for the interests of the membership. Some also work on national standards for their industry, promote best practices for their industry and provide significant networking opportunities.

Most professions have "professional societies" that are dedicated to the professionalism of the career specialties of their members. Local, regional and national groups exist for accounting, human resources, engineering, quality management, sales, and hundreds of other career specialties. Participation in the meetings, webinars, and other activities can be an important source of professional development and camaraderie.

Your personal involvement in either your organization's trade association(s) or your career professional society can also bring you significant career rewards, especially if you are involved in a leadership role. Examples include service on committees, making presentations of successful practices, or even serving on their board of directors.

Steve and Larry became the current chair and the incoming chair of the board, respectively, of a major trade association. They reconnected when they were in the midst of hiring a new executive director to lead the association. Each had risen through the ranks in their companies to become the CEO. They first met 20 years earlier when they attended a two-week industry mini MBA session sponsored by an industry trade association. At that time, both were senior managers, but not yet officers of their companies. Over a period of years, their connection, which began at the school, grew into a strong friendship as they often met at regional and national trade association meetings.

Because both men had been active during their careers in the industry association they were now leading, they set a goal of hiring a candidate for the position of Executive Director—who had also been active in association work. Among the hundreds of candidates who had the educational and performance history they sought, only one also had a strong history of working within an association community. The shared appreciation for the potential of association service for the betterment of their industry forged a bond of mutual respect among the three men, and the candidate with association experience was hired. They believed that together they could move their trade association forward to new levels of service.

Today, all three are retired, but they look back on their decision 20 years ago with satisfaction, because they guided the creation of a much stronger association, one that now helps ensure the safety of thousands of employees and the public each year. The careers of all three men were more successful because they were all well known in their industry due to their association participation.

Demonstrating leadership in industry associations that represent your company has proven to be a strong "get noticed" tool for most of the executives I interviewed. Most trade associations have CEOs and other senior officers on their volunteer boards. Below the board are VP and director-level committees and task forces that might help set the lobbying agenda, promote the industry, develop standards, and provide learning and networking opportunities for member company employees. Your service at a committee level, or even in a subgroup, may filter up to the board, where your boss or your boss's boss will hear of your work. Association volunteer work can also be a great source of job offers from other company representatives who may have seen you perform.

Ned was selected to negotiate on behalf of his industry in a federal government-industry commission created to write new regulations. There was a strong possibility that the new regulations, if they were not crafted with industry input, could cost Ned's company and his industry millions of dollars. There were only 14 representatives chosen from government agencies and industry organizations to sit on this commission. Serving meant a lot of extra work for Ned. In addition to travel to Washington, D.C. every few months over a two-year period, Ned had to network in his company and with those interested parties in other companies in his industry who did not have a seat at the table. When the rule was finally completed, the end result was a sensible regulation. The commission's success, and the relationships that Ned built within the industry, and in his own company, dramatically increased his "get noticed" factor. Eventually, he became the SRVP of Operations for a billion-dollar company within his industry.

<u>Check the resumé of almost any successful executive, and you will find significant community and industry volunteer activities.</u> As an aspiring future leader, you will be well served if you invest part of yourself in both community and industry activities. The satisfaction, relationships, and potential career enhancement are priceless.

10. Find other creative ways to become known and build your professional brand.

Be creative. One manager was taking evening classes toward his MBA. He decided to write all his papers and create his case studies on the company he worked for. He leveraged his need for information for his class work by interviewing various senior leaders in his company. When he finished each school project related to the company, he shared his work with company officials. His process helped him build relationships, and his quality work impressed officials. He established himself as a hard-working, intelligent employee. He is now an officer of the company.

Greg wasn't a particularly great golfer, but he enjoyed playing. He'd heard that "hacker" was the typical skill level in the long-running company golf league, so he decided to join. The company league consisted of front-line people, supervisors, and a few managers from all over the company. Teams of four players competed against each other once a week.

As a relatively new headquarters employee, Greg joined a team, and during the season he played with a variety of people from most of the divisions of the company. When Greg was named to a small task force involving several divisions, some of the golf-league members he had met were also on the task force. Since they already had a connection with him, he fit in quickly and was able to make a solid contribution.

Greg didn't join the golf league to get ahead. But his golfing experience connected him to others in the organization, and it helped him do well on the task force. He still had to prove himself through his work, but eventually his open-mindedness and will-ingness to listen to all sides resulted in a professional brand, or reputation, that he could be trusted by union and management employees. Increasingly higher-level positions and more task force work eventually earned Greg a spot on the management-union negotiating team assigned to hammer out a new contract.

Today, Greg handles all employee-relations responsibilities, includ-ing all union grievances and contract negotiations.

Avoid getting lost in a merger

Most people think of a merger as a career problem. No matter what promises were made in press releases about a "merger of equals" and an open process of putting the new combined team together, the practical fact is that one company bought the other, and one side has the advantage. If your company was the one acquired, it can mean reductions in force (RIF) or fewer new job opportunities, at least for a while.

You have some options. You can keep your head down and hope that no one will notice you, or you can be proactive. Successful executives found that volunteering for a merger integration team, or building relationships with peers in the other company, worked for them. There are no guarantees, of course, but pro-activity usually beats sitting around.

A Promotion Is Not a Reward for Past Performance

A promotion is an acknowledgment that leaders in the organization believe that you have the potential to be successful at a higher level. Past performance is just one indicator of your future potential.

It makes sense, then, that the more successes you have in different areas, the more assurance your senior organizational leaders have that you can increasingly handle more and more responsibility. These successes make you more likely to be in the promotion pool because more of the key people know who you are.

Mentors, Mentors and More Mentors

A computer company Chief Executive Officer (CEO) said it best, *"I do not know of anyone who is really successful who did not have at least one really good mentor."*

"My mentor saw things in me that I did not know I had," explained a female executive. "At one point I worked for him and he took a chance on me by moving me out of my specialty in accounting and into operations management. He pushed me into things I might not have tried on my own. It paid off for both of us. I could go to him anytime, even after he retired."

There are at least three types of mentoring relationships.

1. Formal mentoring programs.

Formal mentoring programs help ensure that everyone at a certain level has a mentor. These programs often assign each participant someone to mentor, too. Both mentoring roles are valuable experiences. The best advice here is to take advantage of any opportunity to get feedback and learn about the organization from someone more senior.

2. Less structured, but intentional mentoring initiatives.

These mentoring relationships can be initiated by a senior person seeking to help develop future leaders for the good of the enterprise, or they can be part of a future leader's goal of getting guidance from a senior person. Sometimes these relationships are formally sanctioned by the company and may even be coordinated by the organizational development department. In other situations, they just get started for a specified period by motivated individuals. In many cases, the relationships can last an entire career.

3. Informal relationships where the word "mentor" is not even part of the conversation, but the relationship works anyway.

Seeking a broader sense of the company from a senior person outside your department, or getting some alternative thinking on a challenge you are facing from another person, can start an informal mentoring relationship. You, too, may find that when you are asked for guidance, a potential mentoring relationship may develop.

The overriding message for you is that you need a mentor, or mentors, to **Get Connected and Get Noticed**. Every one of the executives I interviewed agreed that this is a very important principle of career success.

For a more in-depth look at the role mentors can play in your success, or how you can be a more effective mentor to others, go to the appendix entitled *What Roles Can Mentors Play in Your Success?*

Be a Mentor, Too

Giving back by investing in others is a universal success trait shared by all the successful executives in their interviews. Each benefited from one or more mentors in their careers. As a result, they were willing to be formal and/or informal mentors to others in their organizations.

The positive results for you include:

1. Increased career satisfaction.

2. Helping improve your organization by developing others.

3. Learning from younger employees' perspectives.

Mentoring relationships work best when a "win/win" for both parties. So, when you enter into a mentoring relationship, go into it with the expectation to not only share your insights and coaching with your "mentee," but that you also intend to gain new insights from him or her that will make you a better leader.

One of the key roles of leadership is developing people. Becoming a mentor is a great way to build your leadership skills and reputation.

Social Media Can Connect and Educate You

Increasingly, social media programs such as Facebook and LinkedIn can do more than keep you connected to your friends and family. Both programs have subgroups representing a wide variety of careers and industries. Finding reliable contacts within your organization that might be just down the hall, in a division half way around the world, or even in other companies, can be a great asset. The more resources you can tap into electronically, as well as personally, the stronger your performance and professional brand can be. Even people who you don't know may be willing to help you solve a problem you have at work, if you reach out to them. Consider joining some of the interest groups that relate to your career. Even as a retiree, I stay in touch with my military contacts and with people in the three main industries in which I worked. Some of those contacts helped with content for this book.

Beware, Social Media Can Also Kill or Slow Career Advancement

On your social media sites, you voluntarily provide personal information that is otherwise only available to your friends and family. It is visible to prospective employers, your co-workers and your competitors. What you post, and what is posted about you, can be perceived as negative for your career, depending upon the content.

Here are some social media rules to remember:

1. Whatever you have posted, tweeted or e-mailed is on the record forever and becomes part of your professional image if colleagues and employers check your postings, and they do.

2. Use the Grandmother Rule. Never post anything you would not want her to see. Party photos and other friend postings that are not for Grandma's eyes, shouldn't be on your site.

3. Realize that what your friends post about you on your page affects your brand image. In a way, comments posted about you are somewhat like a "review" of who you are to prospective employers and your co-workers. Your professional brand or image can be negatively affected as a result.

4. Even what you "Like" on Facebook indicates, with up to 95 percent accuracy, your race, gender, religion, and sexual orientation, according to a study published in March 2013 in the *Proceedings of the National Academy of Sciences.*

5. Spending too much time on Facebook and other social media sites during work hours is clearly a negative.

Applying Career Success Principle 1: Get Connected and Get Noticed

Your Quick Guide

This end-of-chapter section can help you in two ways. First, the questions review the key tactics mentioned in the chapter text. Second, you can actually complete the questions for a more in-depth process, to create a mini-action plan.

In what ways can you get better connected? Use this exercise to help you review ways in which you can strengthen your potential brand for promotion, by being better connected and more visible.

A. Getting connected in your organization

___ Join task forces-special project groups

___ Join company-sponsored sports teams

___ Volunteer for company-sponsored community activities such as: Habitat for Humanity team events, clean up days, etc.

___ Get into a mentoring relationship

___ Get connected on Facebook and/or LinkedIn, or blogs with <u>internal</u> networks

_____

_____

B. Getting connected in your community

___ Community service volunteering (What organizations do your senior people support and are active in? What causes are you passionate about?)

___ Local government committees, home owner's association or service clubs, such as Rotary.

___ Church activities

___ School board or school-based volunteering (lectures, coaching, mentoring)

___ Are you connected on Facebook and/or LinkedIn with <u>external</u> networks and interest groups?

_____

_____

C. Getting connected in your industry

___ Industry associations (Which ones are your senior people active in? Depending upon your current job level, a state, regional or national association might be more appropriate. Go to their websites and see what committees and activities they offer.

___ Professional societies (There are HR, IT, engineering and other professional organizations at the state and national levels to be part of.)

_____

_____

What three things can you do in the next six months to increase your connections and awareness level in your organization?

1. _____

2. _____

3. _____

CHAPTER 5

Career Success Principle Number 2: Be a Star Where You Are

Fast Forward  Your Career

Level 1: Establish Your Brand
- Get Connected & Get Noticed
- **Be a Star Where You Are**
- Know Yourself & What You Want

Level 2: Build Your Brand
- Understand the Business
- Be Ready
- Grow as a Leader
- Never Say Never

Make Your Plan and Work It: Update Regularly

If you aren't here to make a difference, why are you here?

Sometimes making the extra effort takes an interesting turn. You may find that you have really put your foot in it, as Gary did.

While heading to Colorado from Wisconsin for vacation with his wife and their dog, Lottie, Gary decided to make a few key customer contacts along the way. After an icy first day's drive they checked in at an interstate motel. Gary's appointment was with a rapidly growing energy company at 8 o'clock the next morning. In the darkened motel room the following day, Gary loaded his briefcase with sales literature and was prepared to head out, leaving his wife and Lottie to sleep a little longer. As he dressed, Lottie got up and stood expectantly beside the motel room door, waiting for an early morning walk. Gary had hoped to leave that to his wife, but Lottie was insistent.

Being the hero type, Gary grabbed Lottie's leash and took her out for a quick constitutional in the icy parking lot. Lottie finished her business and Gary took her back to the room. Now pressed for time, Gary tossed his briefcase on the passenger seat of his wife's older two-seat Honda and drove off.

Arriving at the potential client's headquarters, he parked in front of the imposing six-story corporate headquarters and rushed into the reception area for his appointment.

His plan was to meet the marketing director in the lobby and hand him a brochure, visit a few minutes and take off, promising to come back at another time to make a full presentation.

The security guard called the marketing director to announce Gary's arrival. As the marketing director stepped into the lobby, he said, "Great news, our CEO is in town and he wants to meet you."

The CEO's office was huge, and Gary took a seat. The marketing director sat parallel to Gary. Gary began to smell something odd, and then looked down to see that he had picked up a "surprise" on the bottom of his shoe while walking Lottie. After some small talk, the CEO began explaining what his company's plans were for the next several years. Gary was trying to listen for opportunities to sell his organization, but he was worried that the "surprise" would ruin his visit. It didn't take long before the marketing director began to sniff the air. He sniffed, not as though he had a cold, but more like he smelled something "funny." Gary looked straight ahead, pretending not to notice as the CEO talked on.

Ten minutes later, Gary escaped from the office and headed out the door, thinking, "God only knows what the marketing director thought he smelled." Gary's shoe-borne "surprise" was never discovered. Several months later, Gary returned and, thanks to the effort he made in his introductory visit, he was able to add the prospect to his membership roster.

Being a star often means going the extra mile and going beyond limits to excel.

Pete Kuyper, founder of Pella Corporation, one of America's most successful building products companies, said it best years ago: "It is the extras that make the champions and determine the winners." He encouraged every employee to pay extra attention to detail, to provide an extra bit of courtesy and make the extra effort to live up to promises whenever he addressed his Pella team members.

Here's an example of someone following Pete Kuyper's advice:

Larissa was all about the extras that make champions. She was in charge of a major company meeting that her association planned to hold in Las Vegas. It was the final meeting for her mentor, the president, who was retiring later in the year. She really wanted to make the meeting a success, but the budget was very tight. She enlisted the help of her husband in setting up for the special final evening "Oscar" themed party. They quickly learned, however, that decorating the ballroom for the party was too expensive if they used a local decorating company, so they improvised.

On the Web they found a supplier of decorations for high school proms. The decorations were made of cardboard and would have to be assembled, but the party was only for one night, and they should be fine. Larissa decided to "go for it." The price was right, so she would have more money for other meeting enhancements.

Normally, the low—budget decorations, all of them cardboard with lights and glitter, would be assembled in a gymnasium by excited high school kids from the prom committee. Larissa didn't have a prom committee. It was herself and her husband. Six hours later, all of it spent on their hands and knees, the eight-foot lighted arch was standing in the ballroom, ready to welcome their guests to the organization's version of the Academy. She asked the hotel event staff where they could store the decorations until the following night, the night of the party.

Twenty four hours later, they returned to the ballroom expecting to move the display to the entrance of the room and to put the final touches on the other decorations before heading to their room to change into formal wear.

But where were the decorations?

They found them crushed into a dumpster. The hotel day staff hadn't told the night staff to save them.

After several hours of duct-taping and other creative repairs, the Oscar party got underway, and only Larissa and her husband knew of the struggles they had overcome to make the party a success on the limited budget. The guests had a great time and enjoyed the Elvis and Marilyn Monroe impersonators and the DJ—all added to the program and paid for because Larissa saved money on the decorations. It was a star performance!

Deliver Value

Being a star is about making a difference for the organization wherever you are in your present position. Virtually every one of the 60–plus executives I interviewed for this book underlined the importance of delivering value. Value is another way of saying "making a difference" at every level of your career. The nature of the value that you deliver will change as you move up, but value is the reason you are on the payroll. If your professional brand says you add value, you are already ahead of others.

Early in your career, your value may be the expertise that you brought into the organization and the way in which you personally contribute through your own labors. That's typical of the executives who told me that they came into their organization through HR, IT, engineering, sales, and other specialties. But, as they were promoted to higher level management positions, their "value" to the organization was less about their original technical or professional expertise and was increasingly about their ability to create team value, along with their leadership skills.

It may seem obvious, but failing in your current job, or just getting by, is unlikely to result in a future promotion. So, be a star where you are!

What does being a star where you are really mean?

To begin with, being a star means more than just meeting your current job-performance objectives. Star performance includes impacting the organization and your team mates in ways that are clearly above expectations. Think of the successful managers, directors and officers in your company. What are they doing that identifies them as "stars?"

"If your goal is to get promoted, you have the wrong goal." one executive stressed to me. "I lost track of that concept at one point in my career and as a result, I spent nearly five years in the same job. I always wanted to take on more and more challenges, but I forgot that my job wasn't to impress, but to express myself in accomplishments for the organization. When I took the "crown" off of my head and stopped the dysfunctional thinking that went with the crown, I could focus on delivering value again. Within six months, I received one of the biggest promotions of my career. I finally stopped focusing only on my future and focused instead on my performance. Then my accomplishments spoke for themselves."

How to Be a Star Top 10 List

1. Stars bring out the best in themselves and in others.

Stars inspire those on their team, and they are a positive influence on all the employees in other departments and divisions. They understand that a win for their team that comes at the expense of another team, or the organization as a whole, is not really a win for anyone.

Mark was a division officer. He came up through sales and marketing and understood that achieving the organization's sales and income goals were the key requirements of success for everyone. He felt strongly, however, that "how" a team makes the numbers should also matter. He observed that team leaders who were focused only on their own team's success, often ignoring the needs of other teams or even the company's long-term success, did not contribute as much to the organization as team leaders who improved processes, developed new skills, and supported other teams along the way. Both types of team leaders must achieve the sales and revenue goals, but one team leader has stressed everyone out and emotionally drained team members, while the other team leader built team camaraderie and team member strengths so that the team would be better able to meet the next year's targets. The "How Team" developed stronger team members who put more muscle on their individual skills, capabilities, decision-making skills and, most importantly, future leadership skills. Even the newest "How Team" members learned quickly that "How" matters.

To reinforce the "How" process, Mark tied individual team-member performance reviews and compensation to how they, as team members, delivered total value, not just their sales results. This was a creative way to reinforce the importance of a balanced approach to delivering results. It helped create a very healthy team culture that consistently delivered high-performance results and developed more future leaders. Both Mark and his team members were often singled out for the contributions they were making to the organization beyond meeting sales quotas.

2. Stars help create other stars.

Whether it is mentoring someone over a period of time or just welcoming a new employee into the organization, a star reaches out unselfishly to develop others and help them succeed. The senior management team is always looking for stars who are committed not just to their own success, but ultimately to the success of the entire organization.

Kay was the "architect" of the manufacturing design plans that the sales department sold to clients. She also oversaw all the manufacturing. In other words, she was one busy executive!

The sales team was failing, and the CEO made an unusual move. Instead of naming one of the top salespeople to head the sales division, he chose someone who had less sales experience, but who had more management experience and had exhibited leadership qualities the CEO liked.

For Kay, the decision meant that she would have to invest her time "breaking" in the new sales director by explaining the how's and why's of the design process. It also meant she would have to loosen her criteria for agreeing to make proposals for a while. Normally, she refused to develop proposals unless the potential client was really interested and well qualified.

Kay saw that the new sales director was willing to understand the design process and was appreciative of the time it took to make proposals. She did a few extra proposals for him that did not end up in contracts, but the relationship with the new sales director ultimately led to the most successful year on record.

Kay's willingness to help the new sales director find his "groove" is a great example of how a star can help develop another person, which benefits both the individual and the organization.

3. Stars are "gap fillers."

Stars see gaps in the organization's performance. They step up to take on a new project, or take other action to improve results. Often, this means more work for them. Stars take action anyway, not from a sense of, "Wow, look at me," but because they can see a gap, something that needs doing and is not being done. Such actions are typical of someone who has the best interests of the total organization in mind.

Stephanie already had a lot on her plate. She managed all the meetings and conferences for a major section of the industry trade association for which she worked. She sensed that many of the women who attended the association's meetings lacked an opportunity to network with each other. She believed the women could enhance their skills and contribute more to their organizations if they could connect in some way. She began informal conversations with some of the women in engineering, operations, customer service and other disciplines. Soon, a small discussion group was started and, eventually, the group held detailed discussions and planning sessions. Today, in addition to her continuing responsibility to manage meetings for the association, she also coordinates a national organization of professional women, which continues to grow in membership and value. Currently, the women's network sponsors a national meeting and many webinars and conference calls.

John was already a partner in a highly profitable educational company serving Fortune 1000 companies. He had been an exceptionally successful sales executive, and he brought his closing and relationship skills with him to his current company.

His appreciation of people at all levels made everyone, from the receptionist to the client CEOs, feel special, in a very genuine way. He was always looking for people with potential, and he directly, or indirectly, mentored them in a way that increased their self worth, their skills and, ultimately, their performance.

Darlene was a volunteer on an industry team that wanted to build a new training system that would benefit her company and others in the industry. She had a stronger vision of how her company and her industry could benefit from the expertise of John's company than most of her volunteer team mates from other companies. When work began on the new training system, Darlene's company allowed her to travel with John to make presentations around the country, to create more industry buy-in. John was impressed with her passion and skills. He saw Darlene's entrepreneurial skills blossom. He realized that, with the help of a good mentor, she had a very bright future.

A year later, while the new training materials were in the midst of their national roll-out, John sought permission from his client to hire Darlene. At first, Darlene worked as a subject-matter expert, helping create additional content for the program. But it was clear to both Darlene and John that the new training system would have to be aggressively sold to the industry to make the project profitable.

John believed that Darlene could make those sales, and he offered her the opportunity to become a sales representative. Sales would mean a big change for Darlene. She was accustomed, in her old position, to a middle manager's salary, with regular bonuses and good benefits. John's company was a pay-for-performance organization, where total income could be much higher, but there were fewer guarantees.

John understood the psychological challenges Darlene faced. He began coaching her weekly in one-on-one sessions to enhance her prospecting, proposing, and closing skills.

Five years later, Darlene was the senior vice president of sales for John's company. She had developed so well that John often did not even meet clients any longer until they were already under contract. Darlene had made her big career change, and John couldn't have been happier for her and for the company.

4. Stars must learn the business.

That means learning how the technical, operations, marketing, sales, customer relations, and finance departments work together to make the total company successful. Knowing how your work and that of your team impacts the total company demonstrates that you are a team player capable of making an even greater impact on the company's success.

Joe was a very good design engineer. His boss was not only proud of Joe's engineering work, but he was also proud of how Joe built positive relationships with city government officials.

His boss was shocked when Joe asked for a transfer into the sales department. "Why would you want to work with those crazies?" he asked. But Joe had a plan. He knew that the engineering designs he was creating for customers had to be sold by the sales department. Unfortunately, the current company system did not allow Joe to have any customer contact. He felt that if he could work in sales, on the front end of the design process for a while, he might determine ways to make the sales and the engineering design system work better for everyone. Joe's continuing willingness to move around the company and improve company results ended up earning him the COO job before he retired.

5. Stars learn the organization's culture.

Is your organization's culture risk averse? Does it reward entrepreneurial actions? Is it data-driven to the point that it doesn't move ahead without tons of analysis? Are the key executives all of one mind set, political party, or philosophy? Having a sense of the way in which decisions are made, and who the key influencers are, can be significant when proposing changes to current programs, or recommending new ones.

Suzanne came to her current company from a culture in which people were rewarded based upon their total "victories." In her old company, she had lost a few rounds, but overall, in a baseball metaphor, she was 9 and 3. She had nine clear successes, but she also had three failures. In her new company, however, some of her peers had many fewer victories than she, but they also had fewer losses. They got promoted; she didn't. Why? The culture in her new company was very risk averse. Everyone tended to focus on the things that went wrong. The company culture was very finance oriented, and she did not understand how that culture manifested itself over time.

Suzanne, with the help of a mentor, realized that either she had to accept the culture as it was at the time and adjust her performance by taking fewer risks, or change companies.

6. Stars under promise and over-deliver.

As one CEO put it, every customer or boss likes to be pleasantly surprised by performance they did not expect. If you promise a good value and can deliver great value, everyone is happy. However, if you promise too much and don't fully deliver, no one is happy. This doesn't mean that goals shouldn't be aggressive. It is just a reminder to be clear on what you will do so that expectations are mutually understood.

Cecilia runs a software-development team. She knows that software development and implementation projects are usually over sold in terms of benefits, cost and completion dates. Overruns of millions of dollars and many months are almost the norm.

To avoid the risk of disappointing customers and damaging her career, she asks that her own management and the client take extra time in the early project-planning phase, to add additional milestones to every project plan. She also asks that the design parameters be prioritized at the beginning of the project.

The results for her are very strong. She misses very few deadlines and often will deliver projects under budget, add features, or beat the timeline. That's when she over delivers and delights everyone. She is careful, however, to never create the presumption that she will always be able to exceed expectations.

7. Stars set high goals for themselves.

Stars are never satisfied just meeting baseline goals. Nothing is ever "good enough" unless it is a star's best effort.

Torry knows that when the team goal is achieved, it reflects positively on the whole team and on him as the team leader. But that doesn't keep him from setting additional goals for himself. He knows he needs more background in finance, so he is taking a class in Finance for Nonfinancial Managers. Torry sees that someone on another team is struggling with a new account that he knows something about. He offers to make a joint sales call to the account he knows, to help make the sale.

8. Stars set high standards for their teams and are always ready to support them.

Stars hold themselves and their team accountable. A star is always asking team members, "How can I help you succeed? What tools and resources do your need? Is there a roadblock that I can help you remove?"

Helen has experienced this issue. If you do not hold all team members to a high standard, performance will typically drop and jealousy might result over who is coasting through with less performance. Helen dealt with a tough situation when the mother of one of the newer employees, halfway across the country, was diagnosed with cancer and was placed in hospice. The young employee naturally wanted to be with her mother while she was slipping away. The team was initially sympathetic, but as the weeks dragged on, they became overloaded and were angry about the employee being away from her job. She was not contributing her share. After several ups and downs in the mother's condition, Helen had to put a deadline on how much more time the employee could be away. Stretching to accommodate special employee situations is always a challenge, but consistent treatment was the key for Helen. She would have done the same for any of the employees. Avoiding team member feelings of favoritism is always a difficult problem for teams.

9. Stars are trustworthy.

Through consistent action, stars demonstrate that, when things are tough, they are there for their team members. If the team knows that their star leader will take a hit for them when necessary, the team will get through difficult times more easily. A star is never about blame. When things don't work, the first reaction from a star is not finger pointing or recrimination. The star's focus is on what did not work and how it can be made to work next time. Failure is only a waste when the team and the organization do not learn from it. Sometimes, trying new things doesn't work. Sometimes, celebrating that the team at least tried something new is worthwhile.

Charlie had already dealt with one merger and the inevitable "control" issues that come from the new parent company. Sadly, in the first merger, he had already experienced the assumption by the employees of the new parent company that they were automatically smarter and their policies and procedures were naturally better than those of the acquired company. He had learned to wait them out over the first year without saying too much. Eventually they relaxed and came to appreciate that Charlie's team had learned a few things over time and that Charlie had successful practices that he could share that would help the newly combined enterprise be even more successful.

It was a second merger/take-over that really caused problems. The new owners had over-paid for the acquisition and, as a result, extended themselves, giving the impression to their investors and Wall Street that they could expect major profits right away. The normal annual cost-cutting budget hassle was even more intense as the new management tried to wring profit out of every function. Weekly, Charlie would have to submit another operating budget, with further cuts.

His team began to wonder how long Charlie would continue to fight for reasonable funding. They expected him to cave in to the new organization, if for no other reason than to save his job. Charlie could see the concern on their faces every time he returned from another round of budget meetings.

The latest cuts were still not enough, so in the fourth budget meeting, the new management presented Charlie with its version of his operating budget.

He returned to his team and said, "Thank you for all the creative ways you have come up with to cut expenses. You have innovated, scrimped, and even put aside your own salary increases, to try to support the corporate mandate. Today, I may have cut the budget even further because my position may be empty. I told our new SRVP of Finance that I was done cutting. Any further cuts would endanger our customers and our employees, and unless he was willing to give me a letter stating that he was taking on the responsibility for safety, I would not accept his new cuts."

The room became quiet. The trust they had in Charlie's leadership was not misplaced. His integrity was not for sale.

The company backed down because the new leadership realized that Charlie would not compromise on safety. Sometimes, standing against senior leadership carries a cost. Charlie was pushed into early retirement three years later. If you ask Charlie today whether he did the right thing, he smiles and says emphatically, "Yes." When he mentors, he always advises, "Integrity can never be for sale. If you sell yours, even one time, the next time gets easier and, after that, it is all downhill."

10. **Stars anticipate the future by following the trends and issues in their industry as well as in their own organization.**
The more a star can anticipate the future, the better prepared he or she is to make an even greater contribution. The more a star is aware of both the internal and external challenges his or her company faces, the better able a star is to develop effective responses.

Erin was monitoring the pressure some states were placing on Internet merchants over collecting state sales tax. Given the recession that began in 2008, states were desperate for revenue. She anticipated that as state after state reached settlements with the major online retailers, eventually, her organization would face the same pressure. After further research, she discovered that her company could be held liable for sales tax on past sales, a potential financial disaster for her smaller company. Erin reported her findings to her boss and, ultimately, the chief financial officer decided that she was right. The organization proactively approached its clients, seeking their approval to charge state sales tax on re-sales or to gain a release from liability so that Erin's company would not be financially liable for back taxes.

Applying Principle 2: Be a Star Where You Are

Your Quick Guide

This end-of-chapter section can help you in two ways. First, the questions review the key tactics mentioned in the chapter text. Second, you can actually complete the questions for a more in-depth process, to create a mini-action plan.

1. What three things currently make you a star?

_____

_____

_____

2. What actions can you take to further increase your success in the job that you are in now?

_____

_____

_____

(Think of how you can help create other stars, how you can take on more, how you can set higher goals for yourself and higher standards for your team. Also, think about how you can increase your trustworthiness with your team and the organization.

3. What extra contributions can you make to enhance your star power?

_____

_____

_____

Remember these star attributes:

1. Stars bring out the best in themselves and in others.

2. Stars help create other stars.

3. Stars are gap fillers.

4. Stars must learn the business.

5. Stars learn the organization's culture.

6. Stars under-promise and over-deliver.

7. Stars set high goals for themselves.

8. Stars set high goals for their teams and are always ready to support them.

9. Stars are trustworthy.

10. Stars anticipate the future by following the trends and issues in their industry, and in their own organization.

CHAPTER 6

Career Success Principle Number 3: Know Yourself and What You Want, then Create Your Own Unique Career Plan

Fast Forward ⏩ Your Career

Make Your Plan and Work It: Update Regularly

Every executive I interviewed acknowledged that the farther up the career ladder they moved, the more they needed to understand who they were. Call it self-realization, or one of a hundred other terms, but really effective people continue to grow in their understanding of themselves. I referred to this process earlier when I talked about "becoming," the process of growing.

In the past, Jack had never felt quite as though he fit in with the senior executives of the firm. Many of them had been officers in other famous companies, and most had educations from prestigious schools. Jack had completed college while working full time and had started with the firm as a salesman.

But Jack had become the "go to" guy whenever the company expanded its product line. He had been the one to open new markets with the big-box retailers, often dealing directly with the top brass. He was grounded and had become known for his decision-making skills in a crisis.

The president asked him to "stand by" the morning of the quarterly board meeting. Jack didn't know why. After waiting an hour, he decided to go to the restroom. When he stepped to the sink to wash his hands, he reached for the soap dispenser, pressed down on the plunger and, instead of getting a squirt of soap in his hands, the dispenser fired a blast right into his crotch. In a rare panic, he then reached for a towel and water and rubbed the spot. Now he had foam all over the front of his pants!

What could he do? What if the president called for him right now?

His practical side took over, just as it had many times during his career. He took off his pants, wiped away the suds, held them over the electric hand dryer until they were dry and then put them back on, no worse for wear.

He stepped into the reception area, just in time to see the president come out and wave him into the board room.

He arrived to a warm welcome and a round of applause for the company's newest vice president, the guy with the soap dispenser malfunction.

Accepting his senior role became easier. Jack realized he was important to his company, but he also continued to develop himself. He became a student of leadership, constantly honing his skills. Whenever he took on another major growth assignment, he had people standing in line to volunteer to join him. During his career, he developed more future leaders than any other executive.

"Real growth begins with an understanding of who you are today," said a very senior executive. "For me, knowing who I was at any given point in my career was very important because it allowed me to see what I needed to become to make a greater difference at work, at home and in my community."

The late Stephen R. Covey's second of his famous 7 Habits of Highly Effective People is *Begin With the End in Mind*. He suggests that if each of us does not develop our own self-awareness and, as a result, become responsible for our actions, we allow other people (family, friends, and associates), circumstances, and our own background (training, conditioning, and experiences) to shape our lives by default. Do we want to live our lives and careers intentionally, or let them be guided by default?

If you are serious about creating a really successful and satisfying career, you must be willing to do the "personal analysis and personal growth work" necessary to achieve career success.

Whether you think that a career in management with ever-increasing responsibility is your goal, or you want to continue to grow in your specialty career field, self-awareness is important to your success.

When I say each of us must do the "work," I am not talking about the actual work you are responsible for at your desk or in the field. I am talking about the lifelong "work" of self-analysis, connecting with others, learning, and adjusting. These are the keys to keeping yourself ready for the next level in the organization.

Successful people regularly ask themselves: Who am I today? What skills do I have? What is my motivation? What is my reputation, my professional brand? What kind of person do I want to be, or need to be, in the future? What kind of a brand or reputation do I want to have? How effective am I in working with and leading others?

"While I fully support doing the 'work' of self analysis, I believe there is a potential trap in misusing the concept of 'knowing who you are,'" explained a CEO. "The trap comes if, in 'knowing' one's self, a person stops and says, 'Well this is who I am, and I can't change that.' That is giving up. We can all change. As my executive secretary once said, 'Even the boss is trainable.'"

Even the finest business schools and most engineering, IT, finance, and other professional specialty schools tend to lack formal education offerings in "soft" skills. Sometimes called "people skills," they really are more than that. I believe a fuller mastery of such skills includes the ability to analyze yourself and to get help in understanding your own personality. The higher you go in your career, the more your success in applying management and leadership skills becomes more important than any single professional skill or knowledge you might have. Successful application of leadership principles depends upon the leader understanding his or her motivations, passions and relationships.

Some of your most important career progression work will be on your own, building such skills.

To paraphrase many of the executives I interviewed, *A promotion is not a reward for past performance; it is about the future. It is an opportunity that leaders in the organization believe you can succeed in for the good of the enterprise.* So, while you need to be successful in your current position, success there is only one indicator of future success. Being ready for the next level is an ongoing part of life in management. A major part of being ready is knowing yourself.

Zane was a great listener. He was empathetic, and his people felt they could talk to him about anything. They really liked him, and he felt good about that. He had been on the front line with many of the people he now managed. Tough times put significant pressure on Zane's team to produce more product with less labor per unit. Some of the component parts were now made overseas, and one department in the manufacturing plant was shut down as a result. Zane's team was both angry about that and fearful that they, too, could be outsourced. Zane sympathized with his team's concerns, but he knew that if everyone focused on the outsourcing, productivity would go down and they would all be vulnerable. Zane had to get tough. That wasn't his nature. He had to overcome his need to be liked by everyone and learn that being respected during this tough time was more important. He talked with each team member individually and drew out their concerns, but ultimately he had to tell the team that their mission was to assemble the product efficiently, safely, and with a high degree of quality. Anyone who was not willing to do that had to go, because they would drag everyone else down with them.

The experience was hard on everyone. Zane realized that he did not know much about his own personality traits or leadership style. Was he cut out for higher-level management and leadership roles, or would he be better off in a staff position?

Becoming self-aware involves, in part, being able to answer the following questions about your leadership style. The better you understand your style today, the better able you are to make adjustments or improvements as you seek higher level positions.

1. Do You Suffer From Multiple "Brands" Within Your Organization?

Some people suffer from multiple "brands or reputations" in their organization. Do you know what your brand/reputation is? Your closest co-workers may have one view of you, your boss may have another, and other leaders in the company still another. Your fiercest internal competitors may have another opinion entirely. Which one is real? The truth is, they are all real. And if you don't know how others in the organization see you, you may not be best equipped to function successfully, with them, and your career progression could be hurt.

One executive told me that as a young manager he had been promoted several times ahead of his peers, but then his promotions stopped. During the lull for him, his company scheduled all managers for a 360-degree review. Three subordinates, three peers, and three senior leaders were chosen confidentially by Human Resources to do an evaluation of each individual manager.

The results were a shock to the young manager. On a scale ranging from 1 (meaning promote this person immediately) to a 10 (meaning do not promote this person at all), his results showed a cluster of evaluations around 2 (great news) and a second cluster at 8 (bad news). There were no rankings in between. Obviously, he had a major problem. Even though he had strong advocates, he also had strong detractors. Eventually, the detractors needed to be won over or his career would continue to be blocked.

Even if you think you have a pretty good sense of who you are, it pays to know how others see you. Refer back to **Career Success Principle 1: Get connected & Get Noticed: No One Gets Ahead Without Help** where we talked about mentors—official and unofficial. Mentors can be invaluable "mirrors" to learn how others in the company see you.

You may feel that your lower reputation in some segments of the organization is unfair, because it is based upon one incident or some internal competitor who is jealous. Perhaps you feel that if other folks knew you better, they would have a more positive opinion of you. But fair or unfair, a negative brand/reputation needs to be changed.

How will you handle improving your image and reputation? Complaining about it is clearly not the answer, of course. Most successful executives suggest getting as much input as you can about how different segments of the organization see you, then quietly, but intentionally, take action to improve their perceptions.

Remember the young executive who had very strong supporters, but also some very strong detractors? He understood that, at some point, the negative people would hurt his career unless he could at least turn their opinions from negative to neutral. He assumed that most of the negative comments were from people who were not in his division and probably did not know him well. One of his strategies was to become involved in a multi-divisional task force so that he could work side-by-side with others, in order for them to know him better. When the opportunity came up to be the

United Way Coordinator in his building, he took the extra duty position. The United Way responsibilities allowed him to make presentations to diverse groups within the headquarters building. This exposure extended his network and showed him to be a decent person and a competent manager.

Knowing what your professional brand/reputation is within the enterprise is an exercise in understanding the way in which others view you. Part of your reputation comes from the way in which your personality is perceived by others. As I said earlier, this is your professional brand. Successful people make a special effort to understand their personality traits as part of their continuing effort to become more self-aware. They know that the way in which they act and interact at work is important to their career success. The better you understand how your personality manifests itself at work, the better you can learn to make the most of your strengths and eliminate, or at least mediate, your weaknesses.

Increasingly, your Facebook and LinkedIn presence in social media can add or detract from your professional image. Be sensitive to what you and your friends post online (see chapter 4 concerning how social media can help and hurt your career).

2. What is Your Leadership Style?

There is a direct connection between your personality and your work and leadership styles. Here are some classic styles. They are neither right nor wrong. However, depending upon the situation, one may be more appropriate than the other. Most successful people, while feeling that one or the other style is more comfortable for them, recommend that the higher you go in an organization, the more important it is to be able to adopt different leadership styles, given the circumstances.

Fireman?

If the building is on fire or your organization is in the midst of a major crisis, everyone wants a leader who can take action quickly, one who does not need all of the facts before acting, and one who can get things stabilized ASAP. No committees, no research projects, not a lot of collaboration, just action. The famous case of how a major pharmaceutical company dealt with a product tampering situation is a good example of a fireman response. As soon as a medicine of theirs was known to cause customer problems, even though they were isolated and were due to product tampering, they immediately pulled the product from store shelves nationwide. That bold action ended any further public concerns and their quick response endeared them to their customers.

But, to get their products back on the market, they needed to develop tamper-proof packaging. That took a more thoughtful, collaborative approach--a Farmer style of leadership.

Farmer?

Farmer leaders are always thinking about the future of the enterprise (harvesting), and they take the necessary preparation steps along the way (tilling, planting, cultivating) for long-term success. They are not sitting around waiting for the next fire.

A volunteer board chairman of a nearly 100-year-old trade association of natural gas utilities, and the staff president, could see that increasingly more gas utilities were being acquired by electric utilities. Both men knew that combination gas and electric utilities tend to earn more money from their electric business. The two leaders were concerned that their current gas members' new electrically focused management teams might not appreciate the value of the association because it had been focused only on the natural gas business. That was a significant threat. On the opportunity side, they noticed, that budget "belt tightening" and other common challenges across the electric industry might make the electric side of the utility industry willing to join their association if it were refocused to serve both electric and gas interests.

Relying on their Farmer leadership styles, they envisioned a future harvest of a larger, more economically sound association with gas-only members, combination gas and electric members, and even electric only utility members. Ultimately, it took them two years to create the new organization. As others joined in their vision, the concept grew, and all the necessary steps were taken to make the future vision a reality. It was not an easy path.

Traditional gas members were wary of the potentially stronger influence of the electric members. They feared that they would lose the benefits of their gas-only organization. The electric utilities had no recent history of working closely together at the operating level, so they had to be convinced that joining the expanded organization had benefits that exceeded the cost of added dues and travel expense. They had to see it as an investment in enhanced safety and productivity. Eleven years later, the organization is thriving and new members have joined from throughout the United States. The association is also the largest creator and deliverer of online learning for both the natural gas and the electric industry.

So which leadership style do you rely on most? Do you tend to use the farmer style of leadership or the fireman's? <u>It is important to know whether you tend to be more of a farmer or a fireman today, because the higher you go in an organization, the more important it is to be able to function successfully in both roles, depending upon the situation.</u> Senior executives need to have the ability to make sound decisions in a crisis, while leading the organization forward to improve its processes, so that the need for "crisis" management is reduced over time. Your goal should be to become known as a very effective firefighter when there are fires to put out, but also to become known as a strong farmer, who can build for the future. Knowing which style you tend to be today allows you to focus on developing the other style for the future.

3. What are some of your personality traits: Introvert, Extrovert, Creator or Executor?

Many of the successful people I talked with have developed a pretty healthy sense of their personality type over the years. Learning to be more self-aware is a good thing, they agree, because to constantly improve as leaders they needed to recognize their current strengths and to work hard to fill in where they perceived gaps.

Why is this important? The higher you go in an organization, the more your success rests with the performance of others. Whether you head a department of 10 employees, a division of 200 or a business unit with 1,000, you can't personally do all the work, or even supervise the work closely. You need to be good at delegating work while still maintaining control and accountability. To do that, you need to have great people around you. Part of finding those great people for your team is to know how they think and how they will react to change and crises. That means knowing who they are. If you do not understand who you are, how can you expect to understand others? The best teams are composed of people with diverse thinking styles and skills. To be certain that your team has a successful mix, you must learn what each team member's personality and thinking styles are like.

My purpose in this section is not to get you to become a management consultant, an expert in industrial psychology or your own therapist. But the experts agree, as you build your career success plan using the 7 Principles of Career Success, it helps to know yourself so that you can maximize the process.

Some Basic Tools for Understanding Personality Types and Thinking Styles

Maybe you have done some personal growth work in this area already, and, as a result, you have some sense of your personality traits.

But if you haven't done such work, there are some basic tools that you can use to help you understand your own personality traits and those of team members. One of the most common personality assessments is known as Myers-Briggs. You can use an Internet search engine to find the official site, as well as other sites that offer the assessment and instant analysis. Obviously, your HR department, or a good industrial psychologist can do a great deal more for you, but my point here is that growing in your career takes some understanding of your personality type.

Here's a quick example of how knowing your personality type can help you. If you tend to be more of an introvert (Myers-Briggs), you are not as comfortable meeting new people. You may not be as outgoing as some might like. You may not be a joiner. There is nothing wrong with that, but some people may misinterpret your behavior and assume you aren't very friendly, or you are arrogant and don't care about people. That kind of professional brand/reputation can hurt your career.

Having a sense of who you are and how that might come across to others allows you to decide how you can overcome such reactions when it is important to your career. If you don't understand yourself at this basic level, you may never understand how others see you. A good mentor, or help from your HR department, can help you see yourself as others see you.

In my own career, I had the benefit of an intense set of personality and leadership analyses conducted on me over several months. The goal was for me to understand more deeply who I was, how I appeared to others, and, at the deepest levels, to explore what I needed to do to improve my performance as president of my organization. The analysis was conducted by LeaderSource, a Minneapolis-based organization headed by Kevin Cashman. His book *Leadership from the Inside Out* is a powerful tool that will help you at all levels, but especially as you move to more senior positions. My team leader at LeaderSource was Joe Eastman. Joe began his career as an HR staffer, but by taking control of his career, he was promoted into operations and took over a major field service unit with hundreds of technical employees. He eventually returned to HR and organizational development and became a senior career coach at LeaderSource. Joe, to this day, continues to nudge me toward realizing more of my potential.

Analyzing Your Role on a Team

Team effectiveness can either be enhanced or stymied by the mix of personalities of the team members. In a recent conversation with a senior leader, he told me that he had used the C.A.R.E. Profile with his team members in the fall of 2012.

C.A.R.E. has identified five thinking styles and related roles on a team: Creator, the idea generator; Advancer, the mover of the ideas forward; Refiner, the seeker of ways to improve the ideas; Executor, the implementer of the ideas; and Facilitator, who assists the team in utilizing all of the talents.

http://www.resolutionmanagement.com/Pages/training_resources/C.A.R.E.html is just one of the organizations that offer the C.A.R.E. profile materials. The goal of this strength-preference tool is to determine where you and your team members have individual strengths (data points) in each of the five roles.

Successful teams need strong people in each of these areas. For example, a team of all Creators has a million ideas, but never gets much done because they lack Executors. A team of all Executors wants to go, go, go, but they often do not have the creative ideas required to be successful. Analyzing the makeup of a team can show if it is too heavily weighted with one personality type. If so, a team can seek additional members with different profiles, to create more balance. It also helps team members appreciate the contribution of the other types of people on the team. As a leader, you must understand which of the personality types you are, because it is natural to favor people who are of the same type as you. Too many team members of the same type is a recipe for failure.

In my own case, I was "off the chart" as a Creator, but I was really weak as an Executor. My entire team plotted their data points on clear acetate sheets. Then we overlaid everyone's results and projected them onto the wall. Now, we could see which traits each of us tended to be strongest in. We understood each other much better. I had been frustrated with some team members because they were always bugging me, wanting to know what the deadlines were, what the budget was, what the design parameters were. Once I had an idea and shared it, I wanted to move on and leave the details to others. The Executors were frustrated with me because I was not giving them enough information to enable them to do their jobs. When we realized that this was a common frustration between Creators and Executors, we could be more sensitive to each others' needs and move the organization forward.

Are You Left or Right Brained?

Are you more comfortable with a set of guidelines and direction, or would you rather be free to make things happen your own way? This is another of those personality differences or thinking styles where there is no right or wrong. Depending upon the challenge a business faces, one type of thinking may be more useful than the other. If the challenge is about complying with a complex set of regulations, a left brain orientation might be best. Left-brained thinkers tend to like structure and procedures. If the challenge is to develop a new name for a consumer product, right brainers are likely to be more effective because they like the freedom to create. Which thinking style fits you best?

Both types of thinking are important to the organization. But, like the Farmer-Fireman example, the higher one goes in the organization, the more important it is to be able to apply either thinking style, given the situation. Having a sense of which thinking style you tend to favor today can help you plan ways of building the other style to enhance your long-term development.

Sam became the COO of a large regional company. He started as a design engineer. He was a real left brainer. It was the thinking style that served him well, given the critical work he had to do in designing electrical systems. But as he advanced within his company, he began to realize that if he were to move outside engineering into general management, he would have to work creatively with customers, stockholders, and local community leaders. He needed to develop his "right" brain so that he could find creative solutions that did not have clearly defined parameters. To build his right brain thinking skills, he volunteered to lead a community relations task force, and he became active on the customer service side of a trade association. There he met other engineers who also had a left-brain orientation. He also met some marketing executives who were clearly right brained. As he spent more time with both groups, however, he realized the most effective executives were the ones who could integrate their left-and right-brain thinking and focus their whole brain on the challenges before them. Sam felt that he had some work to do on his own thinking style, but if the other executives could become more creative and use their intuition, along with their engineering and technical skills, so could he.

My local Habitat for Humanity board was struggling with two issues. First, because there was high turnover of staff and board members, their financial records were a mess and they had not had an audit for 14 months. On the other side, they needed to generate donations so that they could build their next home. They needed a very creative fundraising plan. Thankfully, those more left-brained members took on the financial-record challenges and the right-brainers hatched plans for a rodeo, a Bike and Build promotion, and many others. When it came time to vote for recommendations from both groups, the board had to integrate their thinking to make the best decisions for the organization.

Superhero or Socrates?

At the beginning of this chapter, I discussed the differences between pursuing a technical or specialist/individual contributor career path or one more focused on managing or leading people. Perhaps comparing the typical traits of a superhero, versus a famous philosopher and teacher such as Socrates can help you see how focusing on the individual performance/technical side versus the people side can impact your career.

Super heroes can do almost anything because they have powers no ordinary person has. There is no single problem too large or too tough for the superhero to take on. They get their satisfaction from their own personal accomplishments. They often don't have the patience to work with others who might not have the same powers. They are impatient. Some are looking for public recognition, but many are not trying to be heroes, they just like the idea of being in charge of their own success. Often sales, finance, accounting, and legal professionals are the superhero type. Their work is specialized, they often work independently and their results include the big sale, the clean audit, the award-winning annual report, and the successful court case, which are obvious in terms of who is responsible.

Socrates, on the other hand, was always finding "teachable moments," and tended to be in the shadows. He was patient and tried to get those around him to think for themselves, to make their contribution through collaboration rather than individual effort.

It is a tough transition for a superhero to become more Socratic, but if you aspire to promotions in management, being more Socratic is necessary. The transition means your success is no longer just about what you, the superhero, can accomplish alone. In fact, a superhero has to let go of his or her ability to do great work and be recognized for it as an individual if they aspire to leadership. They have to learn to succeed by the collective success of their team. If you seek success in management, becoming more like Socrates and less like a superhero will be very important.

Gene was once a really good electric distribution lineman. He had personally repaired a lot of downed power lines over the years. But now he was the general manager of the whole organization. There was a severe storm and he had crews spread all around the communities his company served. The lights were out, the heat was off, refrigerators were no longer keeping food cold, and hospitals and nursing homes were on standby power. Something had to be done quickly.

Gene couldn't be a superhero any longer, he could only stand by and cheer (like Socrates would have) his team members as they applied their energy and skills to restoring power. He could no longer have the immediate satisfaction of restoring the breaker on the power pole and seeing the lights come on along the block. His satisfaction now came from seeing the system-wide power come back on because he and his team members had trained and practiced for this kind of emergency.

So, unless you have "real" super powers, your career success will depend a lot more on collaboration—the sharing of ideas and opinions. Collaboration begins with a genuine ability to listen to others. Only if people feel really "heard" will they continue to offer their ideas, even if their ideas are not always accepted. Listening is the first part of successful communications. Communication is another of the skills that the executives I talked to said was critical to their successes.

Patrick admitted to me that he had once suffered from the "I've-heard-that-before" syndrome. When his eyes glazed over during a meeting, his team knew that they had lost him. So they quit offering their suggestions and just waited for him to tell them how to move forward. His inability to really hear them eventually hurt the team's performance and, therefore, his. As good as he was, he was not consistently smarter than his entire team. It wasn't until he learned not to assume he already knew the answer that his team's enthusiasm and performance improved.

Paula was "dinged" in her performance review as a poor listener and was an especially poor receiver of criticism. As she moved up and learned some additional skills. She learned that "criticism from anywhere, whether legitimate or not, should be taken to heart and worked on. It makes a difference at 'draft' time," she said with emphasis. Paula had learned how important good communications skills are to future promotion.

Both Patrick and Paula tended to be superheroes. Superheroes don't need to be good listeners. But because both aspired to higher level management positions, they had to significantly increase their ability to listen to and engage their teams. Without the team's full effort, neither Patrick nor Paula will be successful in the future.

4. Do You Love What You Do? Is Your Passion Showing?

Passion is infectious, and it is well worth spreading around your department and your organization. Everyone appreciates working around someone who enjoys what he or she does. Job satisfaction, having a sense that one's job matters, always ranks higher than income alone on employee satisfaction surveys.

Tragically, job satisfaction and positive passion at work is often lacking. In a 2013 Dale Carnegie Training Survey of 1,500 employees, only 23 percent of gen Y employees and 33 percent of millennials and baby boomers reported they were "engaged" in their work. As unfortunate as these statistics are for those un-engaged employees and their employers, the situation presents you with a significant opportunity. Let your passion show. It will be a positive differentiator.

Most executives I interviewed said that having a real passion for their industry, their company and their own work was a key factor in their career success. The occasional mistake or failure will be forgiven or forgotten sooner if there is a sense that you have a real passion for doing good work. If your passion gets lost in the routine of the day-to-day or through burn-out, you may need to move on or rekindle your passion because, as many successful people said, "You can't fake it."

I hope that your interest is piqued by the various ways your personality, thinking styles and passion play into your career success. Self-awareness is one of those subjects that isn't typically part of a college curriculum, especially at business school. Yet executives at the highest levels consistently told me that to get promoted to the very highest levels, they had to understand themselves and those around them at much deeper levels. My primary intent is to get you thinking about the special person that you are. You are truly unique. You have a set of innate and learned abilities. You can develop yourself more successfully, however, if you have a sense of "who" you are today and how you might need to change as you continue to grow professionally.

You are always better off taking some time to consider in which direction you really want to go at different stages of your career instead of just "flailing away." Don't let the old phrase, "If you don't know where you are going, any path will get you there" apply to your career.

The rest of this chapter is intended to help you decide whether you currently prefer the specialist/technical career path (sometimes called the individual contributor) or the management/leadership path. The 7 Principles of Career Success can be applied to successful careers in both paths. Many careers have included movement back and forth between the two tracks. Most three-to-five-year career plans, however, tend to be focused on one or the other path.

Before you decide which path is right for you at this time, you owe it to yourself to think through some key issues. Be careful not to fall into a common career trap that focuses your choice on how much money you can earn. Too many people think that the only way to earn a high income or to achieve high status is to choose the management track. While it may seem like the most common track to a good income and becoming an executive, it is not a path for everyone. There are thousands of highly successful (and very well-paid) people who took the time to think through a version of the questions below and ultimately decided that they were not well suited for the management/leadership track. Continuing to grow in career specialties that were **not** heavily focused on management/leadership was the right decision for them, and they were happier and they were still well paid.

Creating a career plan for yourself begins with some key questions:

1. Is a management/leadership career really for you?

Getting work done through others is definitely different than doing the work yourself. You may be a great field tech, engineer, finance person, salesperson, or IT specialist, but management means letting go of your personal ability to do great work and, instead, you must develop and use new skills to get great work done by others. Can you let go of the security of being a star player and become a great coach instead? Do you really want to let go of your current success as an individual performer now, or in the future, and seek new success in managing others?

2. Are you comfortable with more responsibility in management—and the stress that comes with it?

A promotion means that you and your team will be accountable for increasingly more work. More people will be looking over your shoulder, and other departments will depend on you and your team to perform. If something is not working, you can no longer jump in and "fix" it yourself. The team has to do it.

3. Are you comfortable with how your family and friends will feel about your move into management?

You may have to travel more, and there may be more times when you can't attend your children's school conferences or sports events. Your spouse may have to handle more household duties and arrange your social life. How might your added responsibility affect your spouse's own career? What if you have to physically move your family to another city? Executives have been clear that a supportive family is very important to their success.

4. Do you really enjoy working with others?

A very successful computer CEO shocked a group of MBA students that he and I were mentoring by saying, "If you don't really love people, save yourself a heart attack and stay out of management!" Being a "people" person, one who genuinely enjoys working with others, is a very important trait for a successful management career.

5. Do you know what your present strengths are?

What is your personality like? Are you more of an introvert or an extravert? Are you a detail person or a big–picture person? Can you both praise and give constructive feedback to people when needed? How do you deal with criticism yourself? What are your bankable skills today? As you look upward in the organization, what future skills will you need?

6. Do you see yourself enjoying an increasingly larger role as leader?

Every employee can be a leader in the job he or she is currently in. But crew leaders, supervisors, managers, and senior executives find themselves constantly increasing their leadership skills. Supervisors and managers are organizers of work, trackers of progress, and team-based goal achievers. A leader is one who inspires and is able to challenge people to achieve at their highest potential. It is possible to be both a good supervisor/manager and a good leader, but many executives feel that people tend to be better at one or the other role.

7. Is moving into management a clear objective for you?

For some, the only reason they want to move into management is because they think it is the only way to earn more money. If earning more money is your primary motivation, you may want to rethink your decision. There are other ways to earn more money that do not require the people passion that management requires.

For others, they did not have a specific objective to pursue a management career initially. Over time, however, they found themselves in positions that required strong management skills. As long as they continued to grow their managerial and leadership skills and succeeded, this was the right path for them.

Manuel came into the energy business from a retail background. He had a very clear focus on what he needed to do to earn future promotions in his new industry. When Scott was hired as an engineer, his only initial goal was to be a supervising engineer. Today he is COO. Sharon came from state government as a specialist in HR. Initially, her career vision did not include heading a multimillion dollar customer service function in the operations division. All three employees ended up in senior positions, far beyond the levels they envisioned in their early career plans. That's the beauty of creating career plans at each level. You may see your plan grow into reality because you were proactive, or you may end up with a surprise opportunity. But without your pro-activity, your chances of any promotion are much lower.

Applying Career Success Principle 3: Know Yourself and What You Want, Create Your Own Unique Career Plan.

Your Quick Guide

This end-of-chapter section can help you in two ways. First, the questions review the key tactics mentioned in the chapter text. Second, you can actually complete the questions for a more in-depth process, to create a mini-action plan.

1. At this stage of your career, which basic career track fits you best?

    __ Specialist/Technical or individual contributor

    __ Management/team leader

    Why? _____

    _____

2. Which personality traits most fit who you are today? Mark an X for one trait in each pair.

    __ Fireman or   __ Farmer

    __ Socrates or   __ Superhero

    __ Left Brained or   __ Right Brained

    __ Creator or   __ Executor

3. Go back to the list above and circle the trait that, if you could improve in it, would most likely help you get your next promotion. It may be the trait that is the opposite of the one you checked.

4. What action steps might you take to improve in the trait you selected in question 3? (If you said you needed to strengthen your ability, for example, to be more like Socrates and less of a superhero, you might offer to join a company task force that is working to solve some interdepartmental problem. This would require you to work together with others toward a common goal.)

_____

_____

5. What are you most passionate about at work? What gets you up and coming to work each day?

_____

_____

_____

6. What can you do in the next six months to gain a deeper understanding of who you are today, what your personality traits are like, and what your work style is? (think about taking a personality or work-style assessment, ask for a 360 review in HR, talk to a mentor..)

_____

_____

CHAPTER 7

Understand the 7 Key Principles of Career Success: Level 2

Fast Forward  Your Career

Make Your Plan and Work It: Update Regularly

Each of the 7 career success principles is important at every level of your career. The first three, however, are listed in Level 1 because they can be applied immediately on your very first job to help you get your first promotion. If the people who are making promotion and career advancement decisions don't know you exist or they don't know you are really doing great work in your current position, then you are not likely to be promoted. As someone said in an interview, "It's hard to make a splash in the organization if you aren't in the promotion pool."

Now that you understand the importance of being noticed, and how to be a star in your current job, you can use these principles to help you get future promotions. Even senior managers need to be noticed and valued, or they are not going to be in the promotion pool to vice president. Achieving future success is a matter of applying the principles at an increasingly deeper level, the higher you want to go.

The chapter you just read featured **Success Principle 3: Know Yourself and What You Want: Create Your Own Unique Career Plan.** It was designed to help you determine the direction in which you want your career to head, and where you might want to explore and develop additional skills.

The next section of the book is the introduction to the four Level 2 principles. Let's take a quick look at each principle before we dedicate a chapter to each of them.

Level 2 starts with Career Success Principle Number 4: Understand the Big Picture: Learn the Business to Maximize Your Value. The chapter explores the principle for you and provides a number of specific examples. Essentially, it points out that the higher you aspire to in the organization, the more you need to understand how the organization you work for (or want to work for) works. What makes it successful? How do all the parts work together (you may find yourself promoted someday into a different part of the company)? Who are the customers, the owners and the competition? What are the major challenges that your organization faces (your current job may not be focused there)? What are the industry issues that could affect your organization and, potentially, your future?

Career Success Principle Number 5: Be Ready: Develop Yourself as Though You Were Already at the Next Level.

Which of the following employees is more likely to get the next promotion? One who realizes that the next level in the company requires a much broader knowledge (both the operating and financial parts of the business) and has taken positive action by completing a community college course in finance for nonfinancial managers and found a mentor in operations, or an employee who is very popular and successful in his own department, but lacks financial and operating knowledge and hasn't tried to get it?

As you will see in the chapter, companies no longer have the time to wait for someone to grow into a promotion. Business moves too fast these days. Newly promoted employees have to "hit the ground running." As a result, the more you prepare yourself ahead of time for the next level you seek, the more likely you will be promoted ahead of someone else.

Career Success Principle Number 6: Grow Your Leadership Skills: Organizations Are Ultimately About People. Don't think of yourself as a leader today? Feel that leadership sounds a bit too military, or doesn't seem to fit your vision of the next promotion you want? I understand. Leaders always seemed to be a separate breed when I began my career. Even as a middle manager, I felt leaders were the big guns in business, politics, and the military. I was an idea man, always ready with a creative list of options to solve the problem the team I was on was facing, but I was not the dynamic, follow-me kind of person who people automatically looked to for direction. I was a team player, not the team captain. Slowly, two things dawned on me. As an Army Reserve "weekend warrior," I was promoted to staff sergeant, the highest enlisted rank in my unit. Later, I became an officer and rose to command the unit. In my business career, I was no longer just a bright guy with a bunch of ideas, but now, as in the Army Reserve, people turned to me expecting direction. They depended upon me. In their eyes, I was a leader.

People already depend on you, whatever your current level in the organization. As you grow in technical skills and in managing others, people will increasingly come to you for direction and help.

Leadership is just part of being successful. It is a skill you can learn. This principle is supported by stories about everyday people who found themselves leading. There is an extensive list of leadership traits in this chapter. My guess is that you already exhibit many of them. Choose the ones you need to work on. Grow your leadership skills!

Career Success Principle Number 7: Never Say Never: Get Out of Your Comfort Zone and Capture the "Butterfly Moments." Virtually every one of the executives I talked with looked back and realized that they had made at least one "gutsy" move in their career. Maybe they bucked the status quo. Perhaps they took a job they thought was out of their competency zone. Many physically relocated their families. In all cases they had to move out of their comfort zone. Personal growth often comes from facing tough or difficult times.

"Butterfly Moments" are those times when you have the proverbial butterflies in your stomach. You are nervous, unsure, maybe afraid of looking foolish or making a mistake. Perhaps you have never been in this situation before. You would rather be doing something else or be in a different place. Maybe you are making a speech to an unfamiliar audience. Are you asking for a large budget increase before the managing committee? Has your boss asked you to present next year's plans for your division to the board of directors? Maybe you are just uncomfortable working on a committee.

But what does capturing these "Butterfly Moments" mean, beyond facing the stress? Think of a butterfly expanding its wings and flying for the first time after leaving its cocoon. If you capture your butterfly moments, you will be stronger and more confident. You, like the new butterfly, will also be more likely to be noticed.

Very few people get promoted by staying in their comfort zone.

The application section of the book is in **Chapter 12: Make a Plan and Make It Work.** Remember the very first chapter about Taking Charge of Your Future at Work and not trusting your future to someone else? Chapter 12 is about making your own personal career plan. Use the worksheets to outline your next pro-motion goal. Choose a future direction that will help you achieve your goals. Use the tools to think a few moves ahead. Sometimes, a career move, laterally, in the short run is a faster path upward in the future.

CHAPTER 8

Career Success Principle Number 4: Understand
the Big Picture: Learn the Business
to Maximize Your Value

Fast Forward ⏩ Your Career

Make Your Plan and Work It: Update Regularly

The following hour-long cab ride was just part of the consequences of Matt not taking time to learn the business.

Matt was the new hired gun who knew the ins and outs of a market that the parent company wanted to break into. He really wanted to become a senior player in his new firm. He did not understand the parent company's business very well, but he was bright and had numerous contacts. He could get the parent company principals meetings at the highest levels, with potential clients, but he needed company representatives to sell the company services.

Soon after he was hired, the two company principals asked Matt to arrange client introductions in Matt's hometown, Los Angeles. He knew he was being tested, and he was pretty nervous. Rather than show his discomfort, however, he used his macho personality as a cover. After a typical one-hour L.A. freeway trip, Matt escorted his two new bosses into the executive offices of a huge company. Matt knew the executive VP socially. The parties all sat down in a conference room overlooking a palm-tree-filled park. After an hour of conversation about needs and possible solutions, the executive VP seemed intrigued and said, "Let's see what our union president has to say about how your solution will impact the workforce." Matt's two principals looked sadly at each other. They were a nonunion company and they knew from experience that they would not be allowed to work for this potential client.

Matt should have known. If he had researched the client further or bothered to talk with his principles more about what type of clients presented good matches, he would have saved himself an embarrassing ride back to the hotel.

Matt's mistake was thinking that all he had to do to be successful was to use his current skills as a matchmaker without knowing much about the business. He thought he could be a hero without really understanding the company he worked for. He did not know enough about what they built, how they built it, or how they related to the competition. He thought that providing introductions to new prospects and schmoozing with his bosses was going to be enough.

The higher you climb a ladder, a mountain, or to a new level in your career, the more you can see below you. In an organization, you can see how various parts of the landscape of the organization fit together. At the highest levels of an organization, a CEO must be able to see the interests and the interconnectivity of all the stakeholders–customers, owners, employees, and the community.

In careers, the ability to see and understand the "bigger picture" is important to success after a promotion, but it can also be a critical "leg up" for any candidate seeking a promotion. CEOs need supervisors, managers, directors and officers who not only know their own piece of the business, but how their piece fits in with the total organization.

Pete, when he was an operating manager, sat with his peers in a major budget meeting. There was always pressure to reduce expenses in the operating side of the business, so the pressure was nothing new. His team members knew that more dollars in their budgets meant that they would have more people working for them. This meant they would have more visibility and greater chances for promotion. Anxiously, Pete's team waited, to see how their leader would do in the budget meeting.

Would Pete get his share of the budget? Would he get more? Would he be weak and give away money to another department? Pete's team had agreed that they needed more money for an important and ongoing infrastructure project. But Pete, after listening to all the presentations, from his peers to their boss and the finance division head, shocked everyone by volunteering over $1,000,000 from his team's budget to help another director fund one of her projects. This was just not done in the usual company culture. But Pete did it with a simple explanation. He believed that her project would contribute more in the next year to the overall success of the division and the company than his own project, which could wait a year. His team thought he had "wimped out." But his action showed the senior level team that he understood the big picture, a major sign that he had the kind of broader perspective the company needed and the potential for a strong future in higher level management. He was promoted to VP several years later.

Therese has responsibility for the customer side of the business. She also regularly hangs out with the finance and operations division leaders, and she connects with various team leaders and line personnel informally throughout the company. She listens for ways in which her division can provide information, such as trends, customer needs, and concerns that might affect both the money side and the operating side of the business. She encourages her people to connect, peer-to-peer throughout the company. She invites finance and operating people to meet with customers from time to time so that they understand whom they are all ultimately working for. As a result of this proactive "cross functional" philosophy, Therese and her team are able to make a larger impact on the total company.

Sometimes it is difficult to get a handle on the big picture, even if you are proactive. Other department team leaders are often busy working on their objectives and are reluctant to take the time to explain their function. Occasionally, other departments are purposely not very transparent. Keep at it. If necessary, find another resource, perhaps even a retiree, to help you understand more about how your organization, as a whole, works.

Do You Know Your Corporate Culture?

Another part of seeing the "bigger picture," is understanding the corporate culture.

"The business world and, specifically, your organization is not a perfect place," suggested a chief administrative officer. "There are issues that play out in corporate cultures. Lack of awareness of the organization's 'personality' can make or break your career. Some cultures thrive on risk-taking where not making mistakes is a mistake. Those cultures are seeking the 'big win' and know that there will be failures along the way. Others only remember the failures, so a won-loss record of 2 and 0 is better than a 10 and 3 record in their culture."

"I felt very strongly that my company should have domestic partner benefits. I saw it not as a sexuality issue but an issue of human rights," explained an HR officer. "I assumed that since all my peers were fair-minded, this was a slam dunk. My proposal failed to get any votes at the management committee level." She went to her boss and asked why there was no support. He told her that when a "values" issue comes to the management committee, individual opinions, based upon individual backgrounds, become very important to decision making. This was a piece of the culture that the HR officer had not fully understood. On the next go around, she went to each person individually, heard their concerns, and was able to frame her proposal differently. Instead of presenting the proposal from her point of view, she was able to use different reasoning, based upon her individual conversations with her colleagues before making her second presentation. Ultimately, domestic partnership benefits were approved, with a nearly unanimous vote.

Another executive reflected on a time when his corporate culture changed dramatically. "For 20 years," he explained, "the company focus was on very tight expense control. There was constant pressure to always do more with less money, consistent with safety, of course. Then the financial picture changed dramatically and the company was in a very different operating mode. We were now actively pursuing long-term growth through infrastructure investments." Why was it important for this executive and his team to recognize when and how the culture had changed? "If we were still focused primarily on cutting costs in our division, when the organizational focus is now on reliability improvement investments, for example, we would have appeared completely out of step with senior management, and our careers would clearly have been damaged. I coach my people this way," he continued. "One sure sign of a promotable person is one who can translate the organization's business strategy into operating actions that deliver results. You can't do that well if you are not paying attention to the current culture of the organization."

Here are some suggestions, with a couple of specific examples, for getting a broader sense of what your overall organization and industry is about:

1. Read the public information about your company.

Get a copy of the annual and quarterly reports and the press releases that the company publishes. Most of these documents are on the company website, under "investor relations." Look for business news stories in the media about your company and the industry. Do the kind of research on your company that you probably did when you were looking for a job. Contact a stock broker and ask him, or her, what investors have to say about your company. Like it or not, understanding balance sheets and budgets should not be a foreign language for you.

2. Volunteer to be on a multi-discipline task force.

Whatever the assignment, chances are good that you will build a relationship with one or more peers in other divisions. Listening to their challenges can give you insights into the broader company business.

3. Connect with other employees, in other departments.

See if someone in another division is willing to have coffee or lunch. Talk about sports or the weather, if you need to, in the beginning, but since most people like to talk about their work, you will soon be learning from them. So, without being devious, listen and learn.

4. Find a mentor in another department or division.

Sometimes officers do not like to mentor people in their own division, in order to avoid any sense of favoritism. See if one of the officers in a different division will spend some time with you. Start with one issue you want to learn about, and see if the relationship grows into something more.

5. Learn more about business in general.

Attend a mini-MBA course. These sessions are usually held over a two-to-four-week period at a community college or local university. Or, if you feel that you are so highly focused on your current specialty, perhaps an MBA, or other business-oriented degree, would be a good career enhancer. Since you are already employed, you don't need an MBA or business degree from Harvard or Yale. A degree from your local university or an on-line degree, will help your career.

Todd completed his MBA on a part-time basis while working full time. When he wrote papers or developed project assignments, he chose subjects of interest to various officers within his company. He interviewed them, learned from their insights, got some needed mentoring, and when he was finished he had a school work project that also helped the company. He readily admits that the process not only taught him formal academic skills, but it helped him learn a great deal about his company. It also helped him build some valuable relationships throughout the company.

6. Connect with peers in other industry companies.

By learning how other companies handle their challenges, you can learn more about your industry. You may also uncover ways to improve your own team's performance and, therefore, enhance your overall contribution to your company.

Tom didn't fit the usual profile of an "old school" manager. He was impatient and wanted to make a real impact on his company and his industry. After running into some internal road blocks, he found a new, creative way to get additional resources for his team. He became active in a national trade association that his company belonged to. He wasn't satisfied to just attend their meetings. He began pushing the association into creating services that would benefit Tom's company, and the industry as a whole.

Within a year, Tom and a team from the marketing committee of the association conceived and built a major new employee-training system that all member companies could use.

Through the process, he worked with colleagues from many companies. He also learned a good deal about his industry and how associations operate. He even learned how high-quality, custom-education projects are created. His efforts were rewarded within his company, and 10 years later he was the head of an industry association himself, thanks, in large part, to this experience.

The Big Picture and How You Fit In

Once you have a basic sense of your company and your industry, you can take time to answer the following questions about where you work now and where you might work in your next position.

1. How does your current personal work contribute to your team or department's goals? What constitutes success for you and your department?

2. How does the work of your team or department support other teams and departments? What happens to their success if you don't achieve your goals, or if you change procedures without considering their needs? How does the way you do things to achieve your own success help or hurt other departments?

3. How does the work of your team or department contribute to the overall success of the company? How could you change your performance or the "how" of your work, to make a greater contribution?

4. Who are the key stakeholders of your organization? Who does it serve? How does it derive its income? What are its chief expenses? Who are its competitors? What are the barriers to increased success? Is the organization a leading innovator, or more traditionally focused? What is your company's "value proposition?" Is it to be the low price leader, like Walmart; an innovation leader, like 3M or Apple; or a customer-service leader like Nordstrom's? Who "owns" your organization?

5. What about the industry you are in? Is it growing? Is it high tech? Are there government regulations that are significant to its future? What are other companies in your industry facing? What does the future look like?

There was a time when I was a young sales manager in charge of several appliance stores that were part of a gas utility. The price of gasoline had doubled, and supplies were so tight that people were waiting in line for hours just to top off their tanks. The price of natural gas was also rising rapidly. There was also a lot of national media buzz about future natural gas supply problems. In the midst of the national industry challenges, however, my job was to sell appliances at a profit. It took me a while to realize that worry about future supply, and what was happening to our utility customers in terms of higher gas bills, was slowing sales. Eventually, it made sense. If customers believed that prices were only going up and there might not be enough supply in the future, how could I expect them to buy a new gas appliance? In sales meetings, I recognized that some of my salespeople began doubting there was a future in the gas business.

I had to educate myself quickly about the national and statewide supply situation so that I could support the salespeople in their customer conversations. Ultimately, we added more energy-efficient appliances to our line, which pleased customers and helped keep us profitable.

Remember what one senior officer said, **"One sure sign of a promotable person is one who can translate the organization's business strategy into operating actions that deliver results."** The more you know about your company's organization and business climate, the better you are able to make an impact.

Applying the 4th Career Success Principle: Understand the Big Picture

Your Quick Guide

This end-of-chapter section can help you in two ways. First, the questions review the key tactics mentioned in the chapter text. Second, you can actually complete the questions for a more in-depth process, to create a mini-action plan.

1. What action can you take in the next six months that will increase

your knowledge of the total business environment your organization is in?

    ___ Read the Annual Report, Internet search the company, cruise the investor section of the website.

    ___ Connect with someone from another division and ask them about what their division's challenges are and how your division relates to his or hers.

    ___ Consider a short seminar or a college course (on line maybe?) related to an area of knowledge that is important to your organization that you know little about.

_____

_____

2. What action, or actions, can you take in the next six months that will increase your knowledge of the industry in which your organization operates?

    ___ List at least two state or national trade associations that your organization belongs to.

_____

_____

    ___ After reviewing the associations' meeting agendas, White Papers or lobbying priorities, list three key industry-wide issues.

_____

_____

_____

3. How would you describe your corporate culture (risk averse, entrepreneurial, or ....?)

_____

_____

4. What other background on your company or your industry might help you be more effective on the job?

_____

_____

CHAPTER 9

Career Success Principle Number 5: Be Ready: Develop Yourself & Perform as Though You Are Already at the Next Level

Fast Forward  Your Career

Level 1: Establish Your Brand
- Get Connected & Get Noticed
- Be a Star Where You Are
- Know Yourself & What You Want

Level 2: Build Your Brand
- Understand the Business
- **Be Ready**
- Grow as a Leader
- Never Say Never

Make Your Plan and Work It: Update Regularly

Sometimes career lessons come from unlikely places. Fred thought he had developed himself and was ready to perform at the next level, but he needed a lesson in humility from a Chicago cab driver first.

Fred was ready, really ready, to blow the socks off the selection committee. His final interview was scheduled in Chicago, near O'Hare Airport. He had survived the initial screening of over 200 candidates to become president of a trade association. Fred had adjusted his resume to highlight his association experience and skills. This new position represented a unique opportunity to use all his career experience. It was the perfect match for the next step in his career.

So, there he was, standing on the ground floor, just under the upper level roadway at O'Hare Airport, two hours early for his interview. He had been to O'Hare many times and he knew that there were probably 30 hotels within a few miles of the airport. He waited for the hotel shuttle. After an hour's wait, he started to wilt in the June humidity, and he became nervous about being late for the meeting.

Finally, he hailed a cab. "I'm really sorry to do this," he said, "I only need a short ride, but I will give you $20 if you will get me to the O'Hare Hilton. I know it's pretty close.

The cabby smiled and said, "Get in. Now open the door on the other side of the cab."

"What?" asked Fred, "You said you would get me to the Hilton."

"Open the door and get out," the cabby said. "You have been standing across the street from the Hilton for the last hour."

Fred gave him the $20 and thanked him for this lesson in humility just before his important interview. He might have blown it otherwise. The "Mr. Big Shot" moment made Fred laugh at himself. It helped him relax and take a positive attitude into the meeting. His advance preparation and the lesson in humility helped him feel confident as he walked into the room and faced three senior officers from billion-dollar-corporate members from the association's selection committee. He got the job.

To be in the best possible spot for a promotion, as you know from the earlier chapters, means that the decision-makers need to know who you are, that you are successful in your current position, and that you have made a special effort to understand yourself and the business beyond your own current department.

The next step in applying the 7 Principles of Career Success is being ready for your next position. Have you analyzed your strengths and weaknesses? Are you working on your shortcomings?

If you were the CEO, would you promote you today? What performance concerns would you have about your skills and abilities, as they are today?

What would your team members and other employees within the company say about your promotion? Do you have the kind of relationship with them in which they would cheer you on, or would they be concerned about your performance in the new job?

What will your new peers say about your promotion? Will they see you as an asset to help move the organization forward, or will they see you as a weak link or a loose cannon?

These are good questions to ask your mentor before a promotion opportunity presents itself. These days, few organizations have the luxury of letting you "grow into" a new job. The pace of business is such that you had better be ready when the opportunity arises.

Remember that earning a promotion requires:

1. An open position or other opportunity.

2. Successful past performance.

3. A belief by the decision-makers that you have the potential to succeed and deliver performance in the future.

4. Support of your employees and co-workers.

5. Support of other department heads and officers.

There are fewer promotion opportunities when the economy is soft. During good times, there are more. Either way, the next opening can come quickly--so quickly that you may not have time to "up your stats" so that you can make a splash and get noticed in the promotion pool.

In a recent national study, 71 percent of workers reported that they are regularly searching for their next opportunity as a regular part of their routine. In a growing economy, new opportunities can come very quickly for you.

If you have determined that added education and a broader perspective on the business are part of your development plan, then the sooner you get moving, the better. These are not the types of career enhancers you can quickly add to your resume.

Sherm was one of the sales crew--highly compensated professionals with successful track records in other firms. Each was at the top of his field, selling custom-made software programs to Fortune 1000 companies. Sherm was holding his own as a salesman, but he could see that the company was expanding into HR consulting, financial services, and custom work in the medical field. The two founders were moving on with other interests, and the COO might be spread too thin to also function as the sales manager.

Sherm made a point of hanging out with the heads of the three new divisions at coffee and over lunch. He learned what their markets were, how their services could help customers, and what the competition was for each new division. When the company opened a satellite office on the East Coast, to feature the new divisions, Sherm was the logical sales person to go. After two years of success, he was moved back to HQ as VP of sales--over all three divisions, including his former sales peers. The company leadership realized that Sherm had prepared himself to be ready for the next level, before there was a next level.

Bill went to work after high school and three years in the Army. He knew he had to get a college degree, but the thought of seven years of night school wasn't something he could face after time in the Army. And now, he had a new family to care for. Seven years later, his boss reminded him in a performance review that if he had started his degree program seven years before, he would be done now. Bill thought about how many hours of television he had watched and how many hours of just "hanging out" he had wasted. He enrolled at a community college the next day. Twelve years later, he had both a bachelor's degree and an MBA. Bill ultimately progressed from laborer to vice president. He made it a point to always be ready for the next level, wherever he was in his career.

"Over time, as I achieved more success in school, I progressed at the company too," explained another executive who started in the field. "The sacrifices I made early on have now generated rewards for my family as the years have passed. My kids can appreciate the importance of taking advantage of their school days because they saw me struggle for years in night school to earn my degrees. Finishing school before you start your career can help open more doors earlier."

Additional Education Builds Your Brand Beyond the Added Knowledge

"Getting more education is not just about gaining more knowledge," he continued. "Some employees talk themselves out of more education because they see a lot of the required courses as being irrelevant to their current career needs or position. They miss the point that getting added education also says some very good things about an employee." For example, it demonstrates that the employee:

1. Can tough it out through difficult times.

2. Is goal focused.

3. Starts and finishes major projects.

4. Can balance competing pressures.

5. Has learned how to learn.

6. Is likely to continue learning.

7. Is more confident.

8. Has stronger communications skills.

All of these attributes are important and are the kinds of traits that companies look for in future leaders. In short, getting additional education is more than taking educational courses. It is also about demonstrating your drive, focus, and ability to handle stress.

Taking courses, or pursuing a degree, doesn't have to be expensive. Coursera is a company founded in 2012 that offers over 100 free online courses from Duke, Stanford, Princeton, and Johns Hopkins. Edx is also new in 2012 and it is a collaboration of MIT, Harvard, and the University of California, Berkeley. You don't need to spend thousands a year to help yourself "Get Ready."

One way to look at the entire process of career success is to reflect on the word "becoming." People, businesses and society are always shifting, adjusting and changing. Successful people must also adjust--become. It's about being ready for the future. Core values, like integrity, don't change. But learning how to relate to younger generations, how to use technology, social media, etc., are important to success. These changes require that we pay attention and understand new phenomena. To be ready for the next level, you need to adjust and evolve.

Later in the book we will have a detailed conversation about having a career plan. But for now, it is important to realize that a career plan is always in a state of "becoming" or evolving, too. As you complete the early phases of your plan and you move up in the organization, you may have to adjust your plan as circumstances change. One important part of the career success principle "Be Ready" is flexibility.

Act Like You Are Ready

Another important "be ready" action is to look and act the part of working at the next level. How do the people at the next level act? What do they look like? What skills do they have that you don't have? Who do they hang out with? What do they do in their spare time? What are they doing in terms of community involvement? Your goal in this thought process is not to become a clone of these successful people, but to have a sense of what your next peer group will look like, and how you might fit in.

"I've reinvented myself a dozen times," said a very senior executive, "and I expect that I will do it again. Everyone should know who they are, at any given time, in their career, and compare that awareness with what the next levels of achievement will require. I like to ask myself, and others: 'If you aren't about making a difference, what are you about?' In the case of reinventing oneself, it takes conscious action to be ready for the next opportunity."

"At 34," the executive continued, "I was a highly successful engineering leader in a great company, but I realized that I was "bullet headed" sometimes. I had few soft skills and very little emotional intelligence. I recognized that my great engineering education had taught me the theoretical knowledge I needed, and it gave me the practical, almost vocational school-type experience I needed to outperform other engineers. But, if I wanted a future in management, leading others, I needed to reinvent myself."

So it was off to school for a master's degree in business.

"I took every soft-skills course I could. I wanted to add to the skills that I already had. I sensed that the strength of my future contributions to the enterprise would depend upon more than my own ability to do work. It would depend upon the sum total of the work of any team I would be a part of. That meant that I needed to know how to delegate, empower, and inspire. I also needed to be able to read a balance sheet, or be a great engineer. I actually chose a specific university because they specialized in this type of MBA."

"The people around me were amazed at the transformation they saw in my relationships with people after I finished my MBA. My success at work increased too, and some very good things happened in my career."

The same executive, now in his 50s, recently completed a doctor of education degree, clear evidence that he is still reinventing himself.

"Getting the formal education I felt I needed at key times in my career has clearly been a differentiator for me. But I tell aspiring leaders that in addition to the specific learning that occurred during my studies, the break from the "rat race," the opportunity to reflect on who I was, what the business needs in the future were. Reflecting on how I might impact the future to make a difference was equally valuable. Not everyone needs to get a Ph.D. , but I believe everyone needs to take the time to reflect in order to make a real difference."

How Will You Fit in at the Next Level?

The higher one moves in an organization, the smaller the leadership peer group is and the greater the responsibility the leadership group has for the success of the entire enterprise.

Ask yourself, "Why would the senior leadership group want to add someone like me to their group?" There is only one reason—to further ensure the organization's success, and by association, the leadership group's success. When senior executives are choosing among potential, promotable candidates, they are looking for:

1. **Compatibility**-someone who looks, talks, and acts in ways that will enhance, not detract from, the current leadership group and the organization's success.

2. **Performance**—someone who has special skills and/or a strong track record of success in an area that is considered a good predictor of success at higher levels.

3. **Low Maintenance**—someone who will not be a threat or de-

mand undue attention; someone who will make the current leadership's job easier.

In a way, the promotion process is a little like the way in which pickup basketball teams are formed at the gym. The team captains are looking for ball handlers, shooters, rebounders, and defensive talent. But there may be a number of players with those skills. So, in addition to individual skills, the captains are also looking for people with whom they feel they can work. They want team players who will pass the ball to the open player. They are also looking for players with a passion to win.

In business, just as in team sports, having good individual skills are not enough, especially at the higher levels in an organization. The senior leadership of every organization needs to be able to trust one another to do their individual jobs, along with being willing to put aside self-interest for the good of the organization and the other senior team leaders.

Develop Your Own Replacement

If you are indispensable in your current position, your boss may block your promotion because you can't be easily replaced and his or her job might be harder for them without you. When times are tough, you may think this is good job security, but it is also a trap and can block your next promotion. One sign of a successful executive is the ability to develop people. If you are not developing your own team members so that you can move on, you probably won't move on.

John was the head of accounting. He was a real expert on financial information within the company. He was the kind of manager who succeeded because he knew the answers. But he seldom explained to his team the whys and wherefores of the information he developed. He was focused only on providing the information his VP of finance needed, but tended to be difficult when other divisions needed additional data from the accounting system.

When a new division was starting up, the president asked the finance VP if John could move over and help the new division set up its financial system. Since John was so important to the finance VP and had not developed any viable replacement candidates, the finance VP did not recommend John.

Clearly, John was secure with his finance VP, but who knows where John might have ended up if he had taken the new position. Ironically, two years later the company merged and adopted a new, much more transparent finance and accounting system. The information control strategy that the finance VP and John had in place no longer worked for either of them.

Applying the 5th Career Success Principle: Be Ready, Develop Yourself and Perform as Though You Were Already at the Next Level

Your Quick Guide

This end-of-chapter section can help you in two ways. First, the questions review the key tactics mentioned in the chapter text. Second, you can actually complete the questions for a more in-depth process, to create a mini-action plan.

What can you do in the next six months to apply this principle to your career? Review the questions below and check those you intend to take action on. Use the blanks to fill in specific details. Use the three open lines at the end to add actions that you believe may be better, or additional, to the ones I have suggested.

___ Take an inventory of your education, experience and your appearance. Are you missing something? What could make you a stronger candidate?

_____

_____

_____

__ Need to add some education or training? Register for a class that has the information and the skills you need for your next step.

__ Need some added experience? Volunteer for a task force, a merger integration team, or apply for a transfer (lateral is OK).

__ Does your boss, HR, and other key people, know you are interested in expanding your experience base?

__ Do you have a solid replacement? If not, then mentor one or more of your high-potential team members, to develop them as potential replacements.

_____

_____

_____

CHAPTER 10

Career Success Principle Number 6: Grow Your Leadership Skills: Organizations are Ultimately about People

Fast Forward ⏩ Your Career

Make Your Plan and Work It: Update Regularly

At this point in your career, your primary interest in this book may only be about how to get your next promotion. The job you want may be in a technical area or in an interest area that does not involve managing people. That's fine. Your future success does not have to include managing a lot of people. Effective leadership skills, however, are still important to your future success.

As you move up in the organization, you will be expected, increasingly, to become more and more of a leader, even if the job you want doesn't have a lot of staff reporting to it. When people notice your success, you become a role model. And, as you make a larger contribution to the organization, you will be recognized as a leader, whether you sought that role or not. Everyone at every level can be a leader. Leadership is about helping people bring out the best in themselves for the good of the organization. Sometimes leadership is more subtle. It is about ideas and influence. It is about support and encouragement. Leadership does not mean that you have to be the boss in every situation.

Your Career and Leadership

"There is an ongoing debate in 'success literature' and among senior leaders about whether leaders are born or made," explained a senior executive who has a great track record and who recently earned a Ph.D. "In my experience, a person's DNA—their intelligence and upbringing--can be a source of greatness, but every successful leader must, ultimately, create his or her own greatness. It is a lifelong quest. I do not believe that some people are just born to it."

If you do not see yourself as a strong leader just yet, but you recognize that you want (or need) to grow your leadership abilities, it is important to have a clear picture of what successful leadership is. After 40 years of line and staff business experience, interaction with hundreds of senior executives, and 23 years of military service, I still realize that I have a lot to learn about leadership. To help you, here are my thoughts and those of many of the leaders I interviewed in a concise section.

Top Ten Characteristics of Successful Leaders

1. **Leaders begin with a vision of a better place.**

   As a leader, your vision of a "better place" depends upon where you are in your career. As a customer service supervisor, it could be fewer dropped calls. As a line foreperson, it could be another quarter of no lost-time accidents on your crew. As an HR director, it could be a new healthcare program that saves employee families and the organization money. As a CEO, it could be a major restructuring of the organization to improve customer satisfaction and profits.

   The key point is that a "vision of a better place" is not some mystical thing that is only the responsibility of somebody else. It is the first step for every leader—including you.

2. **Leaders engage capable people by sharing their vision passionately and effectively.**

3. **Leaders make believers out of team members, to the extent that they adopt and adapt the vision and make it their own.**

4. **Leaders inspire individual and collective action, which moves everyone toward a better place.**

5. **Leaders give up personal control and trust the team.**

6. **Leaders live the work ethic and "put others first."**

7. **Leaders take responsibility for failure, learn from it and try again.**

   As one successful president and CEO was often fond of stating when things didn't go as planned, "Somewhere in all that poop [the failure], there is a pony [lesson] somewhere," which was usually followed by, "Loosing is just as much work as winning, but winning is more fun."

8. **Leaders don't point fingers; they take the hit.**

9. **Leaders celebrate the team when victory means a better place is achieved.**

10. Leaders develop other leaders and never stop growing their own leadership skills.

The rest of the leadership traits you will have to learn and practice. Many of them may be intuitive for you, but as the executive with the great track record, and a Ph.D., said, "Leaders are made, not born." You can learn leadership skills.

What Do Successful Executives Look and Act Like?

Mostly, they are just like you. They are hard-working and passionate about their jobs and the organization they work for. They are ethical, decent people, also like you. Although each executive's career path (as yours will be) is unique to their personality, skills, and experiences, they all have one thing in common. They all became leaders. Whether you become the head of HR, IT, engineering, sales or finance, or, ultimately, become the CEO, your leadership skills need to be built and strengthened along the way.

So what is the difference between becoming a successful executive--a lead dog, if you will, and being stuck in the pack?

1. "Becoming" is a key characteristic of successful people.

Becoming is another word for the process of evolving, improving, and applying new knowledge and skills. Leaders are not satisfied standing still, personally or organizationally. They know that customers change, the industry changes, technology changes, and they too, must change. They don't change at the core-value level, but they do change in process, style, and capabilities. Having a passionate curiosity about the business and the world is part of their becoming more skillful and knowledgeable. You don't have to be the smartest person in the room, but you need to be a really good student of what works and what doesn't. Being able to "connect the dots" is part of the senior-level process of creating a vision. Here's the difference between learning something new on your own and leading others. In the first case, you may increase your own productivity 30 percent. But leading your team to a new level can increase productivity 90 percent.

2. Being a "Confident Doer" defines most successful leaders.

Leaders learn that there is a difference between having enough self-confidence to take on an unfamiliar task, ask for help and work your way through a challenge versus acting arrogantly and bullying your way ahead, usually trampling on people in the process. This positive self confidence comes from trying new things, perhaps beginning with smaller challenges at first. But as the executives I talked with became increasingly more successful, just like you will, they built the confidence to move on to much larger challenges.

Confidence also comes from failing from time to time, learning the reason why, and realizing that failure is not the end, but the beginning of new knowledge and skills. Never failing means you are not pushing yourself. Another confidence builder is putting others first. What does the team need? How can we help the customer or the other division? Instead of focusing on your own fears of failure and negative personal outcomes, focus on moving others to a better result and you will build self-confidence. Why would anyone want to follow you if you lack confidence in yourself? In the end, it is much better to have tried and failed than not to have tried at all. With failure comes learning which leads to better decisions, and thus success in the future.

3. The "Vision Thing" is a key differentiator.

If you are stuck in the pack, all you see is the back end of the dog in front of you. A leader is out front heading toward a goal. A leader has a vision of a "better place." But the leader also accepts the fact that he or she is part of a team that must be inspired to do its best work. That means sharing the vision and securing the team's willing cooperation by engaging them in the process. It does not mean being the fastest dog or the strongest dog; it means being the lead dog, leading those around you, so that together everyone gets to the better place. Successful leaders quickly learn that one of the keys for their success was surrounding themselves with team members who were brighter than they and were hungry to "get noticed."

4. Strong people-relating skills are critical to success.

This is another key trait of successful executives. You can't get a master's degree in "people relating." Success requires a combination of skills in listening, speaking and writing. It is also about empathy, openness, and establishing trust. It is about letting go and letting your people be free to excel. As more than one executive has said, "You can't fake people skills. Too many leaders think they have what it takes to build trust, but, if, at the first sign of trouble, the boss starts pointing fingers, trust evaporates." The leader's ability to ask the right questions, and listen with an open mind to answers from all different types and levels of employees, is a key success trait.

"Technology has been extremely useful for our business, and there is more to come," suggested a senior executive, "but technology can also be a problem if it becomes a substitute for personal, face-to-face communication. Just relying on texts, e-mails, and video chats does not build the kind of relationships that will help you make it through a real crisis. Use technology wisely, and not as an excuse to avoid the 'face time' work that builds lasting relationships."

"I really like the relationships I have with employees in all areas and at all levels," explained a senior official. "After getting lots of input, ultimately its my job to set direction and give the team opportunities to develop their own objectives and detailed tactics. I try not to manage them, but rather inspire them and give them the tools to do their best for our customers." The role of leader and the role of manager is often different.

"I appreciate good managers," the official continued, "Some functions need detailed schedules, reporting systems, close monitoring and similar management oversight, but I have always strived to be a leader, one who empowers others."

5. Successful people don't worry about who gets the credit.

This is an especially tough lesson for younger employees on their way up. They are often looking for their first big success, and there is a tendency to make sure everyone knows what they did, how they did it, etc. But the higher one goes in the organization, the more this need goes away. Ultimately, the CEO can claim credit for every success of the organization, but he or she knows that organizational success is not about what they did and when, but how the entire organization performed.

"Sometimes it is really hard not to let key people know what your role was in a big success, but as a leader, building up your people, and letting them bask in their accomplishments is very important. Senior management will recognize the role that you, as leader, played in the success. Promoting yourself can make the team wonder about your motives. Whenever I can, I put my people in front of the senior leadership, to let them explain our plans, or to update them on an important issue. It is good training and is motivating to the team members. It also lets senior leadership see who is out there, ready for the future."

6. Give bad news straight, but remember to point out what is good too.

One of the toughest role changes for any newly appointed leader is how to relate to the employee group you were formerly a part of. Being a buddy by covering for people, or glossing over performance problems, is not being anyone's friend. When giving formal performance reviews, or just giving a quick reaction to performance on a job site, remember that people learn from feedback that reinforces good work, as well as corrective feedback. The sooner you provide feedback, the more likely they are to benefit from it. Remember to reward not only the final result, but the way in which it was accomplished. In addition, it is important to remember when and where to provide constructive feedback. It is never appropriate to do so in front of others.

"Team success is how a leader is evaluated," one officer acknowledged. "Developing people is an important part of leadership. But sometimes, for the good of the team, a team member has to go. That is really hard on the employee and the team, but, in the long run, it is best. A leader has to be able to make that decision."

7. An attitude of "my way or the highway" doesn't motivate for long, but real teamwork does.

Intimidation might work for a drill sergeant with new recruits in the first few days of military basic training, but it doesn't work for long with employees in your organization. When you find yourself in the role of a "boss" you will soon realize that people can't be ordered to follow you. People choose to follow leaders. You need to be the kind of leader who your people will want to follow. A truly successful leader is not only seen as an integral member of the team, but knows how teams work. Being smart about what makes successful teams means being able to read people, to put the right mix of personalities and skills on a team, and being open to ad hoc teams that form themselves to tackle issues that a group agrees needs handling. Most importantly, a leader's job is to empower the team to take action and make decisions. Next, a leader supports them by eliminating road blocks that are hindering success. And, finally, a leader is there to give credit when the team is successful and to shield the team from any negative fallout if they were not successful.

Hank always had people from throughout the company standing in line whenever he was given a new division to head. He was known for developing people A larger percentage of his former direct reports had been promoted than those who worked for other executives. "He is focused on results," one of his key team members said, "like every other officer, but he also cares about how we achieve the results. Too many other leaders use intimidation to get results. The year-end results may be there, but everyone is exhausted, stressed out, and no one had any fun along the way." That old-school Donald Trump "You're fired" leadership style is not sustainable or respected. Hank found that it was important to embrace a pay system that rewarded not only the end results but also <u>how</u> those results were accomplished. By focusing on delivering results through team work, collaboration, and empowerment, Hank ensured not only personal growth and success of each team member, but also growth for the organization. He also created a culture where it was truly enjoyable to come to work. The result was that Hank's company was frequently recognized by Fortune Magazine as one of the top 100 companies to work for.

8. Instill a spirit of continuous improvement that builds on both failures and successes.

One membership organization received 50 percent of its revenue from dues, and the other from sales of products that helped the company members comply with federal regulations. Most similar organizations were nearly 100 percent dues. When sales were good for several years, the organization had extra non-dues money to invest in additional services for members, and the employees enjoyed their bonuses. Then the bottom dropped out of sales because an expected new regulation was delayed. The president realized he had made a mistake by becoming too dependent on sales revenue. All of the employees suffered for the next year.

By learning from the mistake, the president, and teams from throughout the organization, worked to develop a new funding model that was more dues dependent. By improving the dues structure, to allow two levels of membership, they could provide great training options and still have a more consistent revenue source.

9. Lead by example.

This may seem self-evident, but too many leaders, at all levels, do not lead this way. If your people have to work weekends due to a major problem, are you there with them? Are you adding to your skills while you are demanding that your team learn to improve theirs? In some industries, early career promotions often go to the most highly skilled or technically qualified personnel. But, eventually, a leader must let go of being the expert and develop leadership skills instead.

10. Emotional intelligence is part of an executive's core.

This is another successful executive trait that typically isn't taught in graduate school. Emotional intelligence is knowing yourself--being in touch with your own feelings, understanding how others feel, and being able to relate. It is about how trust is built and sustained. It is realizing that the price of "cutting just one corner" can take years of work to repair your reputation and regain the trust of your team.

11. Learning from successful people–dead or alive.

Learning lessons from successful people, dead or alive, is another common trait of successful people. By dead, I mean reading biographies of historical figures. One executive said he learned about perseverance from Winston Churchill--prime minister of England before World War II--who was kicked out of parliament for preaching that war was coming, and then returned to lead England through the war. He also remembers Thomas Edison's perseverance when he failed 9,999 times before inventing the first electric light bulb. Another executive was fascinated by Apple founder Steve Jobs' ability to develop products that didn't only meet consumer demand, but often met a need consumers didn't yet know they had. Successful people read biographies and ask, "How did these people become famous? How did they inspire? How did they lead?"

In addition to "hanging out" with historical figures, "hanging out" with successful people in your company, in community volunteer groups and in service organizations, such as the Lions and Rotary, can also be stimulating and supportive. Why spend time with people who do not aspire to success?

12. Gather people around you who will tell you the truth and who don't always think like you do, or agree with you.

As one CEO related, "It can feel really good to have people always telling you how great you are, but CEOs make mistakes. It's hard to improve without honest feedback. It is far too easy for a boss to adopt an attitude that says, 'I am the boss, so do it my way.'" Avoid having clones of yourself on your team. Find a few "oddball" thinkers and get their thoughts on important issues. Alternative points of view can help the organization avoid repeating mistakes that the "group think" team does not see.

13. Question the status quo: take aim at the sacred cows.

Many executives credit challenging common assumptions, or "We have always done it that way" thinking, with great career success. Sometimes major improvements are the result. Other times, the improvements are more subtle. But being open to divergent thinking can be very career enhancing.

Barbara took over a 100-year-old organization. The staff she inherited was stuck in a customer-service model that wasn't working any longer. For decades, they offered classroom training services that the industry they served formerly counted on. But their industry was reducing head count and was beginning to rely on technology--especially laptops and hand-held devices. Barbara's organization still depended upon revenue from classes attended by field personnel. But fewer industry personnel, and the expense of travel, hotels, and fees for printed training materials, were reducing class attendance and revenues. Barbara's vision of a better place for the organization was providing computer-based online training services. That product would mean many thousands more field employees could benefit from training on a 24/7 basis, without travel expense and time off the job. Her vision was ultimately achieved, with great success for all. Only after a complete change-over of her staff, and the addition of some "alternative" thinkers could the new vision be achieved.

14. Learn from tough times.

There is a tendency to think that executives come from upper middle-class home life and that they grew up at the country club. Executives Jonas and Mack both grew up with single mothers, one in the inner city and the other in a farm community. Jonas had an egg route (think of a paper route, but with eggs instead). Mack had gangs all around. Today, one is the founder and co-owner of a major big box retail chain; the other is a very senior officer in a multi-state utility. Both executives credit surviving those early years with providing the kind of grit it takes to succeed at higher levels.

"I buried two of my men. I will take that experience to my grave," said an officer in charge of hundreds of field personnel. "Even though they did everything right during a major incident, they never went home. That kind of experience totally changes your perspective. I realized even more that relationships are always more important than counting the 'widgets' that were produced that day. From a safety perspective, they did everything right. Still, they died. I am so thankful that my company never allows productivity to come before safety. Sometimes employees are accustomed to doing things a certain way, and while not the safest way, they have gotten by. After that incident, I won't let the old way continue. Even if it takes more time to be really safe, we'll take the time. In the long run, we will still make our performance targets and everyone gets to go home."

Leadership is a skill. Whether you have a track record as a "natural" leader who tends to organize things, chair meetings, and offer your opinions in a group, or you tend to be the quiet one who sometimes feels invisible, you can learn to improve your leadership skills. Our military services make leaders out of thousands of 18-year-olds every year. Some of these men and women couldn't keep their bedrooms clean at home before their training. In a few short months, they are functioning as a cohesive unit operating sophisticated equipment as part of our national defense system, often in foreign countries. Some are leading others before they are 20 years of age, as squad and platoon leaders.

Apply Career Success Principle 6: Grow Your Leadership Skills: Organizations are Ultimately about People

Your Quick Guide

This end-of-chapter section can help you in two ways. First, the questions review the key tactics mentioned in the chapter text. Second, you can actually complete the questions for a more in-depth process, to create a mini-action plan.

1. Whom do you consider good leaders in your organization? Think beyond titles. Who brings out the best in others and seems to get

things done through team effort?

_____

_____

2. What makes this person, or persons, a successful leader? (Scan this chapter and list the leadership skills that your choice in question 1 exhibits.)

2.1 _____

_____

_____

2.2 _____

_____

_____

2.3 _____

_____

_____

3. What can you do to improve your leadership skills in the next six months?

___ Become a more "Confident Doer." Take some risk, make an important decision.

___ Lead by example. Engage others in finding solutions that affect their jobs.

___ Share the credit. Leaders raise up those on their team.

___ Hang out with successful people. Ask for coaching.

Add your own ideas.

_____

_____

CHAPTER 11

Career Success Principle Number 7: Never Say Never: Get Out of Your Comfort Zone & Capture the Butterfly Moments

Fast Forward ⏩ Your Career

Level 1: Establish Your Brand
- Get Connected & Get Noticed
- Be a Star Where You Are
- Know Yourself & What You Want

Level 2: Build Your Brand
- Understand the Business
- Be Ready
- Grow as a Leader
- **Never Say Never**

Make Your Plan and Work It: Update Regularly

Sometimes you just have to do things that aren't comfortable for you. Getting out of your comfort zone, the zone where you have control, and a history of success, is a tough, but necessary career success principle to master. You've heard the phrase "no pain, no gain," when coaches talk about building muscle and endurance in athletes? Well, sometimes it takes a little "pain" such as tackling something brand new, to achieve long-term gain in your career.

Sometimes you "gotta do what you gotta do." Adjusting to the unexpected successfully is clearly a success trait.

Ben was a fairly new architect. His boss felt he had finally earned the right to make a client presentation on his own. Ben wasn't so sure, but he packed his drawings, grabbed his raincoat and headed to the airport for a short flight to Chicago. He was very nervous. He was a perfectionist in his design work, but he had little experience in presenting his work.

The plane landed on schedule. As the plane stopped at the jetway and everyone rose from their seats, Ben caught the left side of his pants pocket on the arm rest and ripped an 8-inch tear, down to his crotch. OMG! What could he do? He didn't have much time to get to the client's office, and since this was a day trip, he did not have a change of clothes with him.

He grabbed his raincoat, slipped it on and exited the plane.

"This will work," he said to himself, "I just need to get to the meeting on time, I'll figure something out."

He greeted his client and the staff who were assembled for the meeting. They offered him coffee and water, and one of them reached for his raincoat. He shrugged them off, refusing everything. As everyone sat down, anxious eyes shot around the room. "Who was this guy? Why did he still have his raincoat on?"

After some stilted small talk, Ben began his presentation. His designs were very good and his explanation of why he had designed the space the way he did met with unanimous approval. The client group relaxed. They were dying to know why he kept his coat on during the entire meeting, but no one asked the obvious question.

With their approval of the project, the business part of the day was a success for Ben. Now that he was able to relax, he could explain the raincoat. He assumed that everyone was wondering about it, so he shared his story. Everyone had a good laugh. Thank heavens for the raincoat.

"I never said never," an executive reflected, "to any job that was offered to me, or to a job that a mentor suggested I should go after. Some were real 'stinkers' in the sense that they required me to be overseas, away from my family, or they were lateral transfers, or my friends thought they were the types of jobs that were not going to help my career. But, in every new assignment, I gained important knowledge, skills and experience."

"Being willing to take on different job assignments plays into several other career-success factors:

1. It gets you noticed by leaders in other parts of the company.

2. It broadens your connections with peers outside your current department.

3. It provides an expanded awareness and understanding of the broader business.

Notice that these three career success factors shared by this executive fit very well with the previous chapters.

At one point, this executive became executive assistant to the chairman of the board. His friends wondered at the lateral transfer to a staff job. "At times, I literally carried his bags. I often felt that my success was all about making sure the limo arrived at the front door on time," the executive laughed, " but I got to spend a great deal of time with the ultimate boss. I could study him, but he could also see me at work. He recognized that I carefully thought through issues, planned ahead, and he liked the way I handled myself. After two years, I was given one of those leapfrog promotions that was immense in my career progression."

"Sure, it was hard to be away from my family for six months and then again for a year overseas. It is always difficult to be away from one's spouse and children. But, on balance, being open to all kinds of opportunities allowed me to make a greater contribution to the organization, and I was a stronger person as a result."

"It is a tenet of mine that no one gets ahead strictly on his or her own initiative. Whatever greatness you achieve, it is never only about just you and who you are. One person has only so much energy, so much knowledge, and only so many hours to work in a day. Ultimately, your greatness is about the collective efforts and achievements of those around you. In a very real sense, your greatness is about the richness of your relationships."

"It is easier to build those diverse and high-quality relationships throughout the company and in the industry, if you have moved around some and have tried new things. I've heard that some great leaders have suggested they are really great actors. They are acting as though they know the future and go speeding forward "beyond their headlights." But they are not acting, really. They are embracing risk. They chose excellence by caring more, risking more, and dreaming more. They expect more from themselves and others than some feel is possible. They also have a sufficient foundation in the organization to be able to push the organization forward."

The founder of a major retail chain said, "It may be a cliché, but you really do have to take some risks in life. We made a lot of mistakes when we were small. That was OK, because they taught us a lot about customers and products. We just kept learning from those mistakes. We were like sponges."

"As we grew, we found that some of our team members became risk averse. They were reluctant to take on new assignments, so we created a 'no risk' job-change program. If you were our best warehouse manager, for example, and we thought you could be an even greater asset heading our customer-service department, you could take the new job, knowing that if either you or management felt it was not working out, you could return to your old position without any penalty or shame."

In most organizations, failing at the next level means losing your job. This executive asks, "Why would we want to fire our best warehouse manager? OK, he didn't work out in the new position. But he is still the same effective person he always was. He has a great track record and runs the warehouse extremely well. Given that many of our people do not have college degrees and have worked their way up, we feel that in creating a safe atmosphere, to take some risk is good for everyone. We recognize that everyone is risk averse at some level. Our leadership team is more comfortable with taking risks, because we have a history of learning from our failures, and overall, we are successful. Successfully handling risk over time builds the courage to take on more."

Another executive remembered changing industries, from retail to energy, earlier in his career. What he lacked in industry knowledge (something he could fix), he made up for with an entrepreneurial attitude. "Even if you try 10 things and only one or two work out, if they are real winners, the organization is better off. Trying nothing new is certain failure." Today, he heads the largest operating division of the company. He got the industry knowledge he needed. His willingness to try new things, learn from "failures" and make the most of the big wins has propelled his career forward.

"Somehow, I never let the fear of not having a job keep me from doing the things in my career I needed to do. I saw too many of my friends, out of fear, hold themselves back from taking on new challenges," reflected one female executive. My father often told me, 'the only risk is to take no risk.'"

Natalia was chosen to take over her company's manufacturing plant in California. Recently acquired, the plant was new to the company. It produced a product that the parent company had never made nor sold before. Since she already felt that she had stepped out of her comfort zone by moving her family and taking the new assignment, her initial work plan was to just settle in, meld the plant into the parent company, and smooth out the inevitable wrinkles. Then, after a few years, she could go back to the HQ offices where she was much more comfortable. But just a few weeks into the new position, she realized that the in-house sales department was not performing well and the overhead costs per sale were killing profit margins. Most of Natalia's competitors relied on distributor sales organizations. She felt that independent sales agents could cover the West Coast territory better, and at lower cost. But that meant laying off the internal sales force within the first few months of her tenure. Let it ride or take action? She made the switch and, while it was difficult for the sales staff and her relations with the whole plant, it worked. The plant became profitable and she made certain everyone got their bonuses. She's back at corporate now as a vice president.

A boss of mine at one point was the VP of sales and he reported to the much older SRVP of marketing. The senior man was very risk averse and, while he tended to want to please my boss and me by approving new ventures, he also wanted to avoid confrontations with the finance officer who was against any additional sales investment. The SRVP's way of dealing with conflict was to avoid making any decision at all. Eventually, my boss and I persuaded him to understand that no decision was still a decision. He eventually understood that our business was changing so rapidly that we would rather have a decision, even one we didn't like, than just be on "hold" indefinitely.

Smart leaders make a special point of rewarding those employees who take calculated risks. "It worked the last five years, so let's do it again," is not the way to move your organization, or your career, forward.

Butterfly Moment for Sang

Sang's boss, the division president, asked him to make the new product introduction presentation to the board of directors. "I can't do that," Sang said. "I am not comfortable with them. I don't know them like you do. Isn't it your job, anyway?"

His boss understood that Sang was having what the boss called a "butterfly" moment. That is a time when we all get very nervous, such as before an important speech, or when we are asked to take on a task we are not sure we can handle. But Sang's boss knew that the positive side of a "butterfly moment" comes when the employee, like a new butterfly just out of its chrysalis, stretches its wings and flies for the first time. He knew that this "butterfly moment" would strengthen Sang and prepare him to reach new heights. The boss told Sang, "I've had plenty of exposure to the board. This is a chance for me to showcase you as a solid representative of the other strong people I have in my division. It will not only be a great opportunity for you, but for your peers in our division. It may even help give the board the confidence to approve our new product plan, because they will see your depth of passion for the project. I'll work closely with you all the way."

Virtually all of our executive interviewees told stories about making some difficult, occasionally unpleasant, choices; or facing other "butterfly moments" on their way to career success. Here are some examples:

1. **Making a lateral move into to a different department or position that will require developing new knowledge and skills.**

   Leaving behind a successful track record is tough. Moving into new responsibility means added stress and pressure. And what if it doesn't go well? Why take the risk, given little or no immediate reward in a sideways move? What will your best friend in the company, or your family, think about such a move? Will it look like you are being shoved aside?

2. **Starting or joining a new division/business unit, or transferring to a recent acquisition, is a big step, but it can be very rewarding.**

   Moving to a start-up business that has no track record means that, in your new position, there won't be any past record of success to follow. Transferring into a recent acquisition means dealing with "their" culture and the natural suspicions they will have about you as a representative of the new parent company. There will probably be long hours. Perhaps you have some perks where you are, like a company car or the special office that you finally earned and which you will have to give up. You will face new stress and anxiety operating in an entirely new and unfamiliar realm.

3. Changing shifts or work location.

Having to drive farther to a new location can disrupt your personal life, especially if you have a family. Working a new shift means changes in sleep patterns, changes in meal times, being less accessible to your family for after-school and evening events. Maybe you will now be on call 24/7.

4. Moving to another city.

Moving your family to a different location can be traumatic. You must overcome your children's fears about losing their friends, prepare your house for sale, find a realtor, deal with strangers looking over your home, and maybe lose money in a down market. In the new location, you have the struggle of finding a neighborhood with good schools, the right house, a manageable loan, and unpacking in the new location. You get the picture. Such a move often puts great stress on one spouse because the other, with the new career assignment, is buried in the new job. Stress doubles if both spouses have careers.

5. Facing change head on.

Even if change means only taking on a few added responsibilities, such as helping a new manager get established or being part of a continuous improvement task force, most people don't like change in their lives. As human beings, we are resistant to change.

Enrique was once a "keep-your-head-down" kind of guy. He was an amazing worker, and his years of experience compensated for his lack of formal education. He was uncomfortable outside the areas that he knew well. Every few years, his multi-national company asked him to move and take a transfer to a new city. Repeatedly, he turned them down, citing aging parents, children in school, etc. Finally, the company said, "Move or resign!" It seemed cruel, but the company's experience was very positive when they selectively moved people around their office locations. More often than not, they found employees grew in value to the company, in excess of the financial cost of the move. Employees who remain in the same position too long become known as "blockers." They block others from gaining experience(s) the blockers are now getting repeatedly. In the end, staying too long in the same position is not a productive situation for either the employee or the company.

Enrique and his family moved away from both sets of parents, to a location three states away. While the transition was difficult at times, both Enrique and his family grew tremendously. New friends, a broader perspective on life, and a new sense of "can do" brought Enrique the confidence he needed to ultimately return to headquarters and a higher-level position several years later.

Bruce was a true technology whiz, a Gen X member who was single with lots of peer friends. His boss, a not particularly technologically savvy individual, asked Bruce to take a lateral transfer into the manufacturing side of the business in order to get a handle on their processes. Manufacturing was the least glamorous part of the business, and probably, the least "techie" too. Bruce discussed the offer with some of his peers at a pub one Saturday night. "Why would you want to go sideways?" one friend asked. "What if you lose your technology edge?" another queried. "What's in it for you?" another asked skeptically. Bruce wasn't inclined to move sideways, especially out of his immediate field of expertise.

But he made one important contact before he gave his answer. He asked to speak to the top technology officer in the company, and the conversation went like this. "Bruce," the officer said, "As a recent college graduate, you have very impressive technology skills. But let me tell you from experience, that there will always be smart people coming to work for us out of school who will have great skills too. As the years pass, you can decide to keep up with them by studying the latest hardware and software tools, or you can focus on how technology is used in the company today and how it can be leveraged to help the company in the future. If you are looking for a longer term career in management, the more you can be a problem solver because you determine how to leverage technology, the less you have to be on top of the latest and greatest technology. You can always hire people who have the latest technology skills as you need them. In my opinion," the technology officer said, "this lateral transfer into manufacturing will position you for a much bigger promotion later."

Bruce listened and took the job. After 18 months in manufacturing, his next move was as the head of a major IT infrastructure change initiative bringing the best of technology to the manufacturing sector of the company.

Whatever "butterfly moments" you face, remember that they can lead to professional growth for you, along with personal growth for you and your family.

6. Acting with integrity, giving honest opinions, even if they aren't what management was expecting, can build a career.

Brenda was originally hired as an engineer, but now she was a director on special assignment. The company saw other similar organizations were expanding into new business ventures, and she and other mid-career "high potential employees" were tasked with studying a new business venture the company was considering. If the new venture proved out, it would mean more profits for the company, a much broader reach, and more opportunities for employees of the company to expand and grow as the company did. In short, everyone was looking forward to the "due diligence" work that Brenda and the team were doing. Even the board was primed.

But after a grueling, year-long analysis, Brenda realized that the new venture was not likely to succeed. Brenda could have hedged her recommendations, allowing the senior management team room to move ahead anyway, but she couldn't do that and be true to herself and the organization. After presenting the complete report, she ended by saying, that as much as she personally wanted the new venture to go forward, and she knew that the leadership of the company did too, she could not recommend approval. The disappointment was clearly evident as she left the room. The group debated her findings, but in the end they realized that she was right. A year later, she was promoted.

Another female executive told this story. "I remember one of my first senior management meetings. I was the new kid in the room. I had to make a presentation to the management group. Before I could even start my presentation, the president made a suggestion about a new program he felt would enhance customer service—my area of responsibility. He wanted my immediate reaction. I was surprised and caught off guard. I was thinking that it was a really bad idea. It would cost too much and wouldn't help. With no time to consider my response, I blurted out, "That's a terrible idea." The room went silent and I thought I was in big trouble. After the meeting, the president called me into his office. I thought *here it comes*. When I walked into his office, he laughed and thanked me for being honest, for taking the risk of expressing my opinion. "I am so tired of everyone avoiding conflict, of posturing. I need people who can tell me the truth." The president eventually retired, but not before this female executive became one of the top four officers in the firm. She and the president developed a strong mentoring relationship that lasted 20 years.

Applying Career Success Principle Number 7: Never Say Never

Your Quick Guide

This end-of-chapter section can help you in two ways. First, the questions review the key tactics mentioned in the chapter text. Second, you can actually complete the questions for a more in-depth process, to create a mini-action plan.

Here are a few more questions for you to consider after reading about Success Principle number 7. By reviewing them now, they might help you capture more of the chapter content and apply it to your career.

1. Have you ever said "never?"

     __ To a lateral transfer?

___ To a relocation?

___ To a task force assignment?

___ To disagreeing with your boss?

_____

_____

2. What do you think the consequences were?_____

_____

_____

3. In what ways might you experience a "butterfly moment" and either take on more risk or do something outside your comfort zone and grow your confidence?

___ Be more direct in meetings. Be willing to disagree when it is necessary.

___ Volunteer to make a presentation?

___ Ask for a special assignment from your boss?

___ Ask for a career review from human resources?

___ Suggest a different way of solving a problem?

_____

_____

4. What actions will you take in the next 90 days to apply the 7th Career Success Principle: Never Say Never?

_____

_____

CHAPTER 12

Make a Career Plan and Make It Work

To begin the process of creating a Career Success Plan so that you can make the most of your potential, we need to talk about what a good plan looks like.

As Denise learned, sometimes the best laid plans often seem to go awry.

She had purposely sought out an opportunity, in sales, as part of her career plan. Her first client was coming to town. She knew that he loved to fish. If she could take him fishing on a lake that was nationally known for great fishing, he would enjoy the day and she would have a whole day to get to know him better.

She found an ad for a fishing service that promised to pick them up and drive them to the lake while she and her client relaxed in a deluxe RV, eating fresh muffins covered with homemade jam, and drinking great coffee. Then, at the lake, they would board a fully equipped fishing boat, fish, and then, for dinner, go to a private area for an outdoor steak fry. After dinner, the RV would return them to the city.

The next morning, the RV pulled up. Wow!

The luxurious RV was actually an old panel truck with a huge crack in the windshield. "What." she asked, the driver, "is this?" He said he was so sorry, but the usual vehicle was in the shop. "But please enjoy the muffins, the jam, and the coffee. It will be a great day," he quickly added.

Reluctantly, Denise and her client climbed into the van. The muffins were good and the coffee was hot. The sun was shining, and the day still held promise.

Denise prayed for a beautiful boat to take them fishing. When they arrived at the marina, they walked by some gorgeous boats, but their guide stopped at a yellow inboard-outboard runabout that was old enough to be in a museum. "Oh no," Denise thought, "not a boat to match the beat-up van!" There was a hole in the dashboard where the depth finder should have been located. It was lying on the floor of the boat! "Here we are. Isn't she a beauty?" the driver asked.

The day didn't get better until dinner time. The "guide" had no idea where to fish on the large round lake, so they just drifted with the wind. The only fish they caught were too small to keep. At least the steak dinner was as good as promised.

Denise, in spite of her plan and best intentions, was embarrassed.

"What a day, and what an impression I made on my client," she thought.

Half way home, Denise and her client were quietly contemplating the day when the client started to smile, then laughed. His eyes twinkled, and he said, "What a day of fishing! We don't have anything like this around Washington, D.C. I am glad I came!" In an unexpected way, the trials of the day brought Denise and her client closer together.

The client is still a client, 15 years later.

On the surface, Denise's plan appears to have been a disaster. Clearly, not all plans work as written. But what if Denise had not planned at all? Her client would not have spent the extra day with her. In a way, the unmet expectations helped her client bond with her. She never lost her cool, and she learned that her client could laugh at unexpected situations. Certainly, there would be some "surprises" in their relationship in the future. They would always have this fishing day as a shared memory.

Making a Career Plan

The first phase of any plan is to create a basic vision of what the end result should be. So the beginning of a career plan starts with your vision of what you want your career to be like. Hopefully, **Chapter 6: Know Yourself and What You Want: Create Your Own Unique Career Plan** helped you refine what your basic career vision or goal is at this time.

Career visions often start modestly and build and change over time. Your vision doesn't have to be elaborate in the beginning.

On graduation day, or the first day of work, your career vision isn't expected to include an intricate plan about how you are going to become CEO in exactly 15.7 years. You shouldn't expect to have all your future career moves already loaded into your "to do" list in your smart phone either. That's a little overkill for most career visions, especially early in your career. On the other hand, don't make the all-too-common career mistake of leaving your future to chance or just "going with the flow" and hoping that your boss or HR will take care of you. If you don't create some kind of clear career vision and plan, and set some basic career goals, your career is not in your hands, but in somebody else's.

Perhaps you were first hired because of your specialist abilities in customer service, information technology, sales, engineering, or accounting. Your first career vision may be to become a supervisor in your current work area. If you already know that you want to be the head of your department, or that you want to move on to be something else, great. The key action is to have some sense of where you would like to be in three to five years so that you can make steady progress toward your vision.

Without a career vision and some basic goals as part of a basic career plan, you may find yourself in the same job you are now in years later. <u>It is much easier to apply the 7 Principles of Career Success if you have a career vision to work toward.</u>

Marcus had a degree in journalism, with some part-time experience in public relations and some coursework in advertising. He was hired to be an all-purpose communications person, by the head of advertising, as a recent graduate of the local journalism school. Initially, he wrote some simple material: news releases, sales brochures and stories for the company newsletter. He looked around and saw other communications generalists, much like himself, in the department, who were also immersed in writing projects.

Marcus enjoyed his writing assignments, but as he looked ahead a few years, he could see that he really had two obvious career choices. He could stay in communications in this company. To do that, he would have to add some experience in advertising and hope to replace his boss in 10 or 15 years when his boss retires. Following this path, his career vision would focus on becoming the overall head of communications in the company, or eventually move to another organization in communications. This type of career vision focuses his career on his specialist skills in communications and is often referred to as the "traditional," "specialist" or "expert" career path. To follow this path, he would develop himself by adding more communications skills. He would network with communications professionals locally and perhaps join a communications group on Facebook or within a professional society.

But Marcus could also follow a "nontraditional" or "generalist" career path. Marcus supervised a group of young people during his college years, when they all worked for a community organization part time. He enjoyed managing others. He also enjoyed observing the leaders in the community organization and in his current company. He realized that most of these leaders were not functioning as experts or specialists in their original career fields. They had given that up to manage people, often in teams. Most of the leaders' time was spent on the people side of things. Managing and eventually leading people in teams might open up promotion opportunities for Marcus earlier than waiting around to replace his current boss when he retired.

Marcus, at this early stage of his career, did not have to make a decision about further specialization in communications or joining the lower-level management ranks. But he was smart to be thinking about both futures.

With his current, general vision of wanting to move ahead in communications, but also keeping his eye open for management possibilities, Marcus set about making an initial career plan that kept his options open. He could sign up for a company seminar on supervision and still get more education in advertising. Let's get a quick sense of what a career plan is and how you can begin to create your own.

Career Plans

Most initial career plans start with the goal of finding a job, hopefully in a field that interests you. If you are working now, you prepared yourself for your first job with an education and perhaps some experience, and you landed a position. Whether you had a detailed plan about what you wanted as a first job, and you majored in just the right educational program, or "stuff" just happened, you got a job that brought you to the point where you are today. So let's start from there.

Now, or sometime later in your career, you will probably have to make a major career-changing decision: Think of Marcus' story. If he decides to pursue the communication's director position, he will need more experience and education in advertising. If he wants to pursue a broader management career, he will need to develop his managerial and leadership skills.

How about you? Do you want to primarily work within your educational or experiential field (accounting, engineering, sales, etc.) and take your satisfaction from your personal work and expertise? Or do you want to manage and lead others so that your satisfaction and performance are no longer based on your own personal specialist or technical work, but now depends upon your team's success?

The following section guides you through this decision process. If you are just starting out, you may want to review these questions and file them away for now. If you are mid-career and currently not managing or leading a significant team of people, you may want to pay very close attention and go through the thinking process that the questions present.

The final key principle of career success is to create a plan of how you are going to move forward. In this section you will see how each of the 7 Principles of Career Success can be applied to your career plan. As you consider them, you can make adjustments to your plan. But for now, let's examine the basic elements of a career plan.

Your Career Planning Tool

1. What is the next **traditional or specialist** career progression from the job, or level you are now in?

Based on the way your department, company, or industry is organized today, what career positions (current job titles) are there? (Look at the folks doing those higher level jobs today in order to help you think this through?) These are the future jobs that you could be promoted into in the next five years, 10 years, or even 20 years.

There are plusses and minuses to growing your career within a "traditional or specialist" career path. On the plus side is stability. You will likely continue to work with people you know and who know you and the work you do.

The down side is, typically, that someone has to leave the company or retire in a position above you before you can move up. You can become blocked. And at some point, even if you reach the top of your department, the next promotion might mean moving beyond your department anyway. That promotion will require you to have a broader knowledge of your company and industry.

Remember, the higher you go in the organization the broader your knowledge of the business needs to be, as discussed in **Chapter 8: Understand the Big Picture: Learn the Business to Maximize Your Value**.

List the most likely titles you might be promoted into if you stay in your current department or division.

_____

_____

_____

_____.

2. What are the **nontraditional or generalist** career progressions for you?

Think about how you might move up in the organization, if you got more experience and exposure in other departments. The more potential paths upward that are available to you, the better. Also, the more senior management personnel who know who you are and are familiar with your work, the better the chance you have for promotion. If you use **Career Success Principle Number 1: Get Connected & Get Noticed**, organizational leaders will already be aware of who you are.

There are things you can do to gain experience and a track record in other departments. Lateral transfers are among the ways. Remember the example of the young engineer, now senior executive, who remembered hearing from his boss, the head of engineering, early in his career: "Why would you want to work with those crazies?" when he said he wanted to transfer to the sales department? That experience helped him when he was a design engineer, because he learned how the sales function worked in his company. Eventually, he became the COO, with both engineering and sales reporting to him.

So think about all the possible paths forward for your career, not just the ones that may seem the most obvious.

List some of the nontraditional titles/positions that might be open for you, or that you are interested in? (Think of positions in other departments that might rank a level or two above you.)

_____

_____

_____

3. Think about your general career progression time table. How soon, and how often, would you like to be promoted in either your traditional career path or the nontraditional path?

Your plan should be flexible, because things change. But having some sense of how long you want to be in any one position can help guide you when presented with career-decision options.

Several executives quipped, "Some people may have thought I couldn't hold a job because I moved around a lot in the company." These executives, however, had an advantage. By gaining experience, adding knowledge and building new relationships more broadly inside the organization, they leveraged these positive career enhancers and they were promoted ahead of their peers. They also suggested that, if actual job transfers are not available for you at this time, other tactics such as volunteering for task forces, community volunteer positions, or loaned executive opportunities, etc., can also be helpful career enhancers.

However, these executives warned that staying too long in one place may cause you to be dropped out of the promotion pool and to be overlooked. Being in the same place too long may also cause you to lose your edge, by falling into a routine that does not produce your best work.

4. What added education and experience do you need to make yourself more promotable?

As part of your plan, you need to be clear—and a mentor or two can really be of help here—about what added education and experience you need to make yourself more promotable. Lacking a mentor, a trip to the organizational development department, or hiring a career coach, can help. And, tap into your social network for advice.

Equipped with some outside guidance on how you are perceived today (your professional brand) and what kinds of traits, skills and knowledge higher-level positions in the company require, you are better able to determine how to make yourself more promotable. Add the specific actions you are going to take, and work them into your timetable.

Maybe you need to broaden your business skills. Is an MBA or a mini-MBA important? Do you need to work on the customer side of the business for a while, in order to gain that perspective? Whatever added qualifications you feel you need or your advisers suggest you need, will take time to acquire. Fit that into your plan and discuss it with your family. This application is part of **Career Success Principle 5: Be Ready: Develop Yourself & Perform as Though You Were Already at the Next Level** and **Career Success Principle 7: Never Say Never: Get Out of Your Comfort Zone & Capture the Butterfly Moments.**

5. Let others in the company know of your interest in future opportunities.

Be sensible, of course. Announcing that you intend to be CEO might not be the way to start a new job right out of school. While your current boss, or the head of your department, might want to support your career goals over time, they may also feel threatened by your ambition, or feel that you are not satisfied in your current job. Use common sense, be a star where you are, but, it is not only OK, but necessary, to let others know you are interested in additional opportunities.

To actually make your own career plan, see the next section.

At this point in your career-planning process, you may find that reflecting on the 7 Principles of Career Success (use the Table of Contents for a refresher list) will help you focus on how to apply the principles to your career plan. That's what the next section is about.

CAREER PLANNING

Worksheet & Check List

If you own this book, you have permission to make copies of this Career Planning Worksheet & Check List. Use it to make a variety of potential career plans. Don't be afraid to do some "what if" thinking. Make at least one plan for the next logical promotion and another for something in a totally different area of the organization that interests you.

1. What is the title of the position you want to have, or be promoted to, next?

   _____

2. How soon would you like this change/promotion?

   _____

3. Check below whether your next promotion will be in a "traditional" position in a career path based upon your current skill set and in your department or division where you are well known, or will it be a position in a "nontraditional" career path where

you do not have a history of success yet, but believe you have the potential to do well in?

    __ traditional career position

    __ nontraditional career position

4. Do the decision-makers concerned with this position know who you are? __ Yes __ No

5. Do they know you are interested? __ Yes __ No

   If the answers to either of the questions is no, you need to get better connected and noticed (Principle 1 in Chapter 4). Here are things you can do to become better connected and noticed.

    __ Find a mentor. The person I will ask to be my mentor is _____.

    __ Volunteer for the following task force or committee: _____.

    __ Get involved in the following industry organization: _____.

    __ Connect with the following peers outside my department: _____.

    _____.

    _____.

    __ Become a company-sponsored community volunteer in the following activity:_____.

    _____.

    __ Share my career plan with: __ boss __ HR co-workers __ social network

6. Are you a star where you are? (**Success Principle 2, Chapter 5**)

List three things you need to do to improve your success in your current position.

1. _____
2. _____
3. _____

List some "extras" that you do, or can do, to increase your star power beyond just meeting expectations.

_____

_____

List the name or names of the future "stars" you want to help develop.

1. _____ 2. _____

Trust is one of the most important attributes of "stars." If you need to improve your "trust factor," list two things you could do.

1. _____ 2. _____

7. Anyone seeking a promotion should learn more about his or her organization and the business and industry in which it operates. The more you understand about where the money comes from, what the products are and who the stakeholders are, the better able you are to make a larger contribution. Check off those tactics you have already used and underline the ones that you intend to use in the future. (**Success Principal 4: Understand the Big Picture, Chapter 8**)

___ Research your company and your industry online.

___ Have a conversation with other leaders in other parts of the organization, to learn what they do and how what you do relates to their success.

___ Learn about your organization's culture.

___ Attend seminars or seek formal education to learn skills important to the overall organization, to broaden yourself.

___ Attend industry conferences or meetings.

8. Are you ready for the next level? Promotion opportunities won't wait for you to get ready. This section can help you plan for what you need to do to be ready for your next promotion opportunity.

What education, training, or experience do you need to become a stronger candidate for your next promotion?

Education	Training	Experience
_____	_____	_____
_____	_____	_____
_____	_____	_____

Where can you get this added education, training or experience? (Be specific.)

_____

_____

Who have you selected as your potential replacement?

_____ (It's hard to move on if you are indispensible in your current job.)

Will you fit in at the next level? Do you look the part? Are your language (grammar and/or English as a second language), terminology, and work style compatible with other people working at the next level? _____

_____

Specifically, what do you need to do to demonstrate your readiness for the next level?

____ Wardrobe: What clothes do you need to wear to fit in?

_____

_____

____ Work Schedule: Do you need to adjust your work habits?

How?_____

_____

____ Personal Issues: Do you need to improve your grammar, speaking style, terminology, office organization, posture, hygiene, or any other item that might not fit in well in a new, higher-level position? If so, what, specifically?

_____

_____

_____

9. Are you open to real change? (**Career Principle 7: Never Say Never: Get Out of Your Comfort Zone & Capture the Butterfly Moments, Chapter 11**) Company policies, procedures, and traditions can only guide employees. The more senior you are, the more you will face crises and challenges, where you and your team must determine the best path forward. That will take flexibility and the confidence of having faced tough situations successfully in the past.

List three situations in which you demonstrated flexibility in the last 12 months, or could demonstrate flexibility in the next 12 months. (Think job transfer, applying procedures creatively, taking on a new project)

1. _____
2. _____
3. _____

If you were asked to relocate in order to move your career along, what things, if any, would prevent you from accepting the move?

1. _____
2. _____
3. _____

What concerns would you have if you were offered a promotion into management, where your future success would depend upon team performance, rather than your own personal specialist or technical expertise?

1. _____
2. _____
3. _____

What, if any, relationship problems do you have at work, and what can you do about them?

1. _____
2. _____
3. _____

9. Self-awareness is important at all levels, but it is critical at the highest levels in any organization. Getting to know your personality traits, along with your thinking, and leadership styles, is part of becoming more self-aware. (**Success Principle 3: Know Yourself & What You Want: Create Your Own Unique Career Plan, Chapter 6**)

What self-awareness tools have you used to understand yourself more deeply?

     __ Myers–Briggs or other per-
sonality trait assessment

     __ C.A.R.E. Profile, or other think-
ing style assessment

     __ Worked with a mentor

     __ Worked with a career coach or psychologist

What did you learn about yourself, and how might you want to change, in order to make a positive difference in your career?

1. _____

2. _____

3. _____

If you haven't done this type of self-analysis, what are you going to do about it, if anything?

1. _____

2. _____

3. _____

What part of your next promotion will be especially difficult for you? (Consider workload, stress, impact on family, further development requirements.)

1. _____

2. _____

3. _____

What are your motivations for seeking this promotion?

1. _____

2. _____

3. _____

Now that you have completed this Career Plan Checklist and considered some of the action steps you identified, use the one-page Career Success Action Plan to make a specific plan to get your next promotion.

CAREER SUCCESS

Action Plan

Promotion sought: _____

Goal date for promotion: _____

1. What **Get Connected and Get Noticed** actions do you need to take, and when do you need to take them, to be a viable candidate?

    1.A Who do you need to talk to so that the right people know that you are interested and qualified for the position?

    _____

    When are you going to do this? _____

    1.B Is there anyone who might try to block your promotion?

    Who? _____

    What can you do about this, and when? _____
    _____

2. What actions do you need to take to make yourself more attractive for the promotion?

   2.A   What additional skills, knowledge or formal education do you need?

   _____

   _____

   How soon?_____

   2.B   What can you do to improve your "Star" quality?

   _____

   _____

   2.C   Are there any other actions you need to take?

   (Think of the other Career Success Principles)

   1. _____
   2. _____
   3. _____

Tell somebody--your boss, HR, your mentor, your social network-- that this promotion is important to you. Remember, no one gets ahead without help.

CHAPTER 13

Have Some Fun, and Don't Take Yourself too Seriously

Just two weeks after starting his new position in the private sector, Robert, a former state government official, invited his two new bosses to the state capital. Robert was accustomed to being driven around town in a government car. He met the two founders of the company at a downtown hotel for breakfast. His reputation as a "mover and shaker" in the state capital was the main reason he was hired. The company wanted to expand its sales into state government, and Robert seemed to know everyone. The three of them hailed a cab, and Robert sat in the front seat. He told the driver to take them to the State Commerce Department. The driver said, "You've got to be kidding." Robert, dressed in his formal three piece suit, barked at him, "drive!" The driver drove around the block and then stopped. Robert was prepared to bark another command, when he realized that the Commerce Department was in the building next to the hotel they had just left. Robert had never paid attention to where anything was located. It was his driver's job to know such things.

Embarrassed in front of his new bosses, Robert shoved open the front door of the cab and angrily swung his right leg out of the car door, only to see his blue pinstriped suit leg split, from his crotch to his knee. He looked down at his leg and saw the white skin of his thigh staring back at him. His leg looked like a bratwurst that had overheated on a grill and split along its entire length.

No longer presentable, and in the middle of downtown, Robert had to find a tailor shop to repair his pant leg. Not the most auspicious beginning for the new hired gun!

Sometimes we all take ourselves too seriously. Business requires serious and sustained effort for sure, but when we become caught up in our own importance, we can lose track of our customers and our employees.

Signs of Success

I once worked for two very successful entrepreneurs. Each had achieved significant success personally, and together they had created a great new company that I was proud to be a part of. Earlier in their careers, clients expected to see lots of "bling," signs that the two men were really successful. Gold Rolexes, matching Porsches, tailor-made suits, and razor haircuts were a regular part of their persona. But in the new business, our client base changed over the years, and more conservative client representatives were coming to our offices. Some were put off by the signs of the founders' success. Sometimes those signs actually worked against us when we presented the cost side of our contracts. Some of us started to park our older family cars in the front of the building so that the founders' new sports cars weren't visible to potential clients coming in for talks. Eventually, the founders caught on and called a company meeting. They showed up in tattered clothing, unshaven. We all laughed. They got the message and they understood that their roles had changed. I will forever appreciate the fact that they were not threatened by the shift in the business. They were the type of leaders who took great pride in growing their employees along with the business.

Here's a "Mr. Big Shot" moment I have to confess to. When I was head of heating and air conditioning sales early in my career, part of my job was to maintain good relationships with the contractors I hired to install units sold to customers. One of the contractors was about my age, and he had young twin children, as I did. We also shared an interest in hunting and fishing. We enjoyed our occasional lunches together at various suburban locations. We could catch up on business and personal interests at the same time. One lunch meeting I will never forget was held at a restaurant called the Tremont Plaza, a place he had heard good things about.

Just after receiving our "Juicy Lucy" burger, a parade of young women walked past us dressed in see-through lingerie. We looked at each other, a little embarrassed that we didn't know the show was part of the lunchtime menu. OK, my credibility may be on the line here, but really, I didn't know.

As we munched away, the parade stopped, with one woman standing right in front of our table. What little she was wearing was pink. I looked up and she looked down, and she said, "Ric, haven't seen you since prom. The contractor looked at me as I blurted out, "Darlene, I like your outfit; I mean, you look great, I mean it's good to see you, too." With that, she turned and followed the other models out of the room. My contractor friend just grinned. We ate at Wendy's the next time we met.

"Hair" Was More Than a Musical to Me in the 1960s

Fairly early in my career, I was going bald quickly. My hair never seemed to grow back from my Army days when we were shaved every week. It wasn't yet cool to shave your head in business. Most people had long sideburns and bushy hair. I felt I looked older than I was with my nearly bald head. Some people had elaborate comb overs, where it seemed that six long hairs from the side of the head would be wound repeatedly around on top of the head to give the illusion of hair.

One of my employees moonlighted as a salesman for a hair replacement salon (also known as a toupee palace). After a lot of nagging, he talked me into getting a "rug." You don't need to know the details of how a good hairpiece is made, but the short course is this. The color should match your natural hair along your neck, and the length should be something like the way you normally style your hair.

I showed up at the next management meeting with a head of hair that looked something like a San Francisco Giants football helmet. It was huge and it was golden. Think Jerry Lee Lewis, or a white guy's Afro. I will forever be grateful to the company president, who greeted me, looked me in the eye and shook my hand. My friends were over in the corner nearly sick from laughter.

It's OK to laugh at yourself. Whenever I started to get a little too "puffed up" about myself and thought that I was really amazing, somehow fate would tap me on the shoulder with an experience that brought me back to reality.

Just for fun, go back sometime to the beginning of chapters 4, 5, 6, 8, 9, 11, and 12. Each begins with an embarrassing story of an executive, and a career lesson.

What Makes Work Satisfying (Fun) for You?

The difference between having a job and having a profession isn't about how much money you make, what you wear to work, or what your title is. I believe everyone can view their work as a profession if you enjoy what you do and are constantly looking for ways to improve yourself and the experience your customers and fellow employees have when they are around you.

Doubt me? Let me tell you the story of two 80-year-old shoeshine men in Cincinnati. They work in the lobby of a downtown hotel. I met them one day while I was in town to meet with the president of a company headquartered there. I had time to kill and they did not have a customer at the time. While they put a shine on my shoes, they asked me about my business, how I got where I was, and what my satisfactions were. They wanted to know if it was hard on my family when I travelled so much. I watched them first clean my shoes and then find just the right shade of polish. Then I watched one of the men reach into a can for his secret ingredient that made a new shine last longer. I left uplifted, not only by my shoeshine, but by the engaging professionals I had just encountered. There was a life lesson in that experience that I have never forgotten. Anyone can be a professional. It is about attitude, pride and performance.

"If you do not enjoy going to work, at least most of the time, you are probably not in the right job," said an executive who started his career, right out of the Army, shoveling coal. After seven years of night school and a variety of successful jobs in the company, he became a vice president. I met him first after he had just buried two of his outside workers who were killed while on duty trying to save others. When he said, "Over the long run, it is really important to find a match between what the company needs done really well and your passion to deliver for them while enjoying every day." I knew he had found his right place.

"My two greatest satisfactions as a leader," a senior female executive explained, "are to excel in contributing my team's part of the organizational goals and in developing my people along the way. My father taught me to be accountable for results and to do whatever it takes to achieve them. But as I rose in the companies I worked for, it became apparent that I could no longer do everything myself. Since I needed great performance from those around me, the least I could do was to help them grow. It continues to be a great source of joy for me."

"I have a great passion for my work," a female entrepreneur offered. "Work is a major part of my life, and I actually value that. I realize that some employees are really concerned about a 'balance' between work and life, but there is a common misconception about what blending work and life means. It doesn't mean you ignore your family, your church or your own well being and just work, work, work. It means finding work where the ethics and passions in your life are in sync with your work. Given the hours we all will spend working, it is important that we find work that is satisfying and is consistent with who we are."

"You have to love what you are doing, because your livelihood is on the line," added another entrepreneur. "Passion for the business is critical. Part of that passion is not letting the business outgrow your skills."

"Having fun at work for me," says a 20-something working in New York for a very creative technology company, "is not about achieving a position or a job title. I love what I do because I can soak things up, study the core of the problem, and have a team of intelligent people around me who can generate a really innovative solution on projects that matter. Ultimately, I'd love to be part of a market interrupter, creating something so innovative that it touches consumers in ways they have never been touched before. These kinds of innovations don't just happen. It takes the right kind of environment. I have heard that Google requires that their employees spend 20 percent of their time on new, innovative thinking or learning. 3M has had a similar approach to innovation for many years. I'd like to be in that kind of environment."

Larry Winget, the trademarked "Pitbull of Personal Development" and the author of *Shut Up, Quit Whining and Get a Life* and *They Call It Work for a Reason,* plus many other books and audio programs, is also a highly paid keynote speaker and television personality. The last time we were on stage together, he stuck a toilet plunger on my head. It matched his.

Be careful who you get on stage with!

This is a man who does not take himself too seriously and is not reluctant to make others part of his fun. Is he serious about making the most of his career, "you bet!" Does he have a good time doing it, "you bet!" I consider it an honor to have been crowned by Larry. He inspired me to eventually appear as Elvis, King Richard of Camelot, the Amazing Ricardo, Teddy Roosevelt, a Tucson cowboy, and a 1905 costumed swimmer in the charity dunk tank at company functions.

Bill Butterworth, a keynote speaker, said at a conference I attended, "Life has three stages to dance on: schooling and career development; working and contributing; and life enjoyment/retirement. Too many people treat these as linear. You do one, stop that, and move on to the next. Why not dance every day on all three stages? Learn, grow, work, contribute, and enjoy every day, if you can."

Career success and satisfaction don't come just because you work hard and try your best. Why would you work for 30, 40, or 50 years without knowing how to make the most of your career?

Applying the 7 Principles of Career Success is not being selfish. They are not ways to manipulate your way to more promotions. These are not tricks. If you use them, not only will your career be more successful and you will be more satisfied, but your organization will be better off, too. Applying each career success principle means that you are a better employee.

My own dad is someone who could have used these principles in his career. He came out of World War II and worked 60 and 70 hour weeks as an accountant for a large firm. He believed that his hard work and his accuracy would help him grow in the company and provide a better life for his family. When he retired, after 41 years with the same company, he had raised his family's standard of living far above that of his parents. As proud as I am of what he accomplished at work and in his life, had he known and applied these career success principles, he could have come closer to fulfilling his full potential. He sensed things such as the value of additional education. That's why he supported his wife's efforts to earn bachelor's and master's degrees. That's why he pushed my brother and me into completing our college educations. But there could have been a lot more for him. We never lacked material things. But for his sake, I would have wished for him to feel the satisfaction that comes from becoming, as the United States Army slogan used to say, "Be All You Can Be."

Don't sit back and trust that the winding road of life will get you where you want to be by the time you retire. You can **Fast Forward Your Career.** Take charge of your future at work, and apply the **7 Principles of Career Success.** Not everyone will. Even if every employee were taught the 7 Principles of Career Success on their first day of work, only a few would remember them and apply them.

Your future really is in your hands. Make it be what you want it to be, for your sake, and for the sake of your family, and your employer. Please!

APPENDIX A

What Roles Can Mentors Play in Your Success?

What roles do mentors play?

Role 1: Mirror

Effective mentors often serve as a mirror, reflecting the way in which others see you. It is human nature to "hang out" with people who like you—who see you probably as you see yourself. But the higher one goes in an organization, the more important it is to have a sense of how other individuals and groups in the organization see you.

Susan recalled a time when she was the youngest supervisor, the youngest manager, and the youngest director in the company. She was well on her way toward becoming the youngest officer in the company. But to get to the next level, the senior VP, her "sponsor" and greatest cheerleader, needed the support of the senior vice presidents (SRVPs) of operations and finance. Susan's mentor let her know in very direct terms that she had an image problem outside of her SRVP's sphere of influence. Operating and finance peers did not know her well, and some of their people were suspicious of her success. The few interactions they or their people had with Susan had found her "too ambitious" in their minds, and the "buzz" in their divisions was negative about Susan. Consequently, Susan's SRVP was not going to have support from his peers unless she built a much more positive relationship outside her division. With the assistance of Susan's mentor, she eventually created the trust relationship that she needed to make it to the next level.

Role 2: Thorn in the side—burr under the saddle

Complacency can sideline a career. When your career seems to be moving along fairly well, why take risks? But even if you just need to catch your breath after a challenging period, giving off a vibe that says you are coasting can be detrimental. A really good mentor will push, cajole, or "butt kick," if necessary, to get a mentee to take the kind of actions that are necessary for continued growth and future success.

Hank, the sales manager, was frustrated with two peers in marketing. One headed advertising and the other public relations. Both men were 20 years older than Hank and, in his opinion, they had become lazy and avoided any kind of risk. Hank needed creative communication support for some major customer initiatives, and after numerous attempts to get the help he needed from the two men, he hired freelancers to create the kind of communications he needed. In frustration, he tossed the work he had commissioned outside the company onto the conference table during a joint staff meeting, which included both his VP and several others. The room went silent. Hank's red-faced peers were clearly livid. Hank's boss tried to calm things down as the staff meeting ended. But the meeting wasn't over for Hank.

One of the officers from another division who had observed the incident asked Hank to stay after the meeting ended. Hank knew the officer but did not have a close relationship with him. And the officer had no involvement in marketing issues. After sitting down, the officer looked at Hank and asked, "Do you realize what you just did?" With a blank expression, Hank stammered, "Well,

I probably upset a few people, but I am tired of not getting the support I need from these guys."

The VP said, "Hank, everyone in the room already knows that these two guys are going to work for you someday. Until today, they did not like the idea very much, but now their worst fears are confirmed. You just demonstrated that, in your mind, they are incompetent and you don't need them. What you did wasn't your best career move, because now you have two enemies who, along with their buddies, will try to derail your career." Previously, Hank had never thought of the officer as a mentor, but he was aware that the officer had noticed his potential. Even though it hurt to be confronted, and Hank was embarrassed, he eventually realized that he had received the kind of direct advice that he needed to hear.

Hank and the officer never directly agreed to a mentoring relationship, but Hank was smart enough to check in with the officer often. Over time, with some guidance from his unofficial mentor, Hank learned to be more upfront with people he needed things from instead of going around them. His directness and passion for the organization's success became infectious, and even some of the most reluctant colleagues came around.

Role 3: Cheerleader

Sometimes a mentor sees potential in a mentee that the mentee does not see in himself, or herself. The challenge for some mentors is to help mentees see their own potential, and help them set a course toward achieving the success they are capable of.

Kathy was doing very well as a staff expert. She had moved from a position in government into a position in business at a director level. She was building a solid reputation in her specialty as someone the line divisions could count on. Her mentor, however, felt that she had the potential to be a very senior leader in the company. But that meant that Kathy had to earn her stripes in the line organization.

It also meant that her mentor needed to encourage her to take a lateral transfer into an area that she knew next to nothing about.

She would have to give up, at least temporarily, all of her hard-earned staff expertise and titles. Even her advanced degree would mean little when leading a crew of linemen out in the field. With her mentor's encouragement and support, she "sucked it up" and went to power pole climbing school. "When you are 40 feet in the air, hanging onto a power pole," Kathy reflected, "you have an entirely different sense of what the business is really about." Ultimately, she served as president of one of the operating companies before returning to be one of the top four headquarters officers of the parent company.

Role 4: Coach

Even a star player can improve. The right coach can help fine tune one's game. In sports, a good coach might suggest a slight change in your back swing or a new grip that could make a real difference in performance. So it is in one's career. Having someone whom you trust point out ways to be even better can be a major benefit.

Alejandra received help from her mentor during a merger. She was already successful, but he helped her see that in the new, larger organization, her tendency to micromanage, especially when results were absolutely critical, would no longer work for her. She had to trust her people to do well. Her mentor realized that Alejandra wasn't 100 percent sure they were ready. Her mentor helped Alejandra determine what help her people needed for success, along with ways in which she could help them grow. In turn, she learned how he was handling the legal and government-relations side of the business. These important insights helped Alejandra improve her team's performance, and the contact with her mentor also increased Alejandra's understanding of the broader aspects of the business.

Scott had an advanced degree and was a rising star in manufacturing. He could look forward to being a project manager in a year or two. He had a good shot to become the head of the design team in five years. His mentor sensed, however, that staying in manufacturing might not be enough for Scott. Scott seemed to be looking for a broader perspective on the business, along with more income. That career track meant succeeding first as a sales rep, then in sales management. It also meant leaving a guaranteed salary with bonuses for a small base salary and a commission on his sales. The mentor also knew that Scott's wife was a homemaker with two young children at home. You can imagine the internal struggle Scott was facing. His mentor became a tremendous sounding board.

Even after Scott made the move, he questioned his decision. Month after month, for an entire year, he did not make a sale. The sales cycle was long, (nine to 12 months), because everything that the organization designed and built was unique to each customer's needs. The typical sale was over $1,000,000.

There were times when even the mentor thought he had given Scott the wrong push. But the move eventually paid off with sales. Today, Scott is an entrepreneur and runs his own research, design and manufacturing company. He would have been successful in his original specialty, because he had the intelligence and drive, and he already knew the technical side of the business. But it was his eventual success on the sales and financial side of the business that uniquely positioned him for his current success.

Mentors and a Word of Warning

Mentors are not clairvoyant, nor are they infallible. Ultimately, you are the one who has to weigh their advice and observations, and leverage it as the advice seems to fit you. If you have a trusting relationship, great, but only you can manage your career.

If your current mentor, or one you would like to connect with, has been highly successful in his or her career, by all means learn as much as you can. But it is a mistake to try to become a clone, copying the philosophy, habits and, even in the extreme, the mannerisms of mentors. As one executive said, "As much as you admire someone you know or have read about, just copying habits and actions will not work. You must be authentic. You can't fake it. By all means, learn from others and emulate some of their traits, but your greatness must come from your core. Get help to determine what your weaknesses are. Know your strengths and reinvent your-self, growing into an ever stronger and more effective person."You are a unique person with your own personality and talents, and you will be more successful when developing your own style.

Sometimes, even the most trusted mentor can actually hold your career back. It can be an honest difference of opinion or a little human jealousy, but several executives reported that their mentor, or sponsor, tried to block their promotion at various times. While not a common experience, the successful executives often reiterated that you are ultimately in charge of your success.

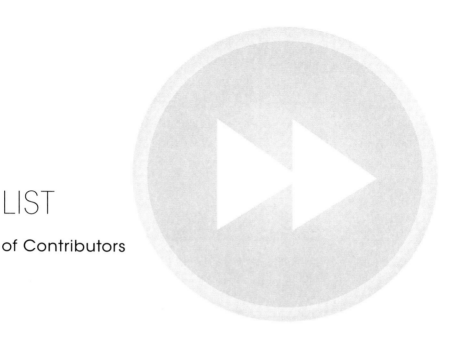

LIST
of Contributors

Over 60 individuals, all of them highly successful in their careers, shared their time and insights with me in individual interviews between 2006 and 2013. Because so many of these generous people have continued to move forward in their careers since our interviews, their current titles and companies may have changed. Therefore, I have decided to simply list the name of the company they worked for at the time of the interview. Each made it clear that their willingness to share their career success lessons with me was in the spirit of assisting others, not in lifting themselves up. This book would not have been possible without the generous sharing by these highly successful people. The content of the book, any omissions, errors, or other shortcomings are my own, however, and not those of the interviewees.

The contributors' resumes include high level employment with Apple, Ameren, Aramark, Black Hills Energy, CenterPoint Energy, Chesapeake Midstream Partners LP, City Utilities of Springfield, Consumers Energy, Commonwealth Edison, DTE Energy, Duke Energy, EN Engineering, Holmes Corporation, HOM Furniture, INTREN, Indianapolis Power & Light, Itron, Inc., Joe

Eastman Assoc., Kansas City Power & Light, KS Energy Services, Lampert Architects, MidAmerican Energy, Midwest Energy Inc., New Mexico Gas, Nicor, an AGL Resources Co.; NiSource, NorthWestern Energy, Omaha Public Power District, Pella Corporation, Integrys, Piedmont Natural Gas, Q3 Contracting, SEMCO Energy, SENSIT Technologies, Space 150, T-Mobile, Broadway Dept. Stores (Macy's), US Forest Service, US Surgeon General, United States Army, Vectren, Victoria's Secret, Xcedex, Xcel Energy and Leadership coaches: Gary B. Cohen, Joe Eastman, and Theresa Lewis.

Book Resources:

The following book titles were mentioned to me during my interviews as being especially useful to career success and development.

Patrick Lencioni (short reads, but very focused help for aspiring leaders) *Death by Meeting, The 5 Dysfunctions of the Team, The Three Signs of a Miserable Job,* and *Silos, Politics and Turf Wars*

James C. Hunter, *The World's Most Powerful Principle, How to Become a Servant Leader*

Jim Collins, *Good to Great*

Kevin Cashman, *Leadership from the Inside Out*

Steven Covey, *The 7 Habits of Highly Successful People*

Gary B. Cohen, *Just Ask Leadership: Why Great Managers Ask the Right Questions*

Michael Porter, *Competitive Advantage*

Bolman & Deal, *Reframing the Organization* and *Leading with Soul*

Hammer and Champy, *Re-engineering the Corporation*

Craig Neal, Patricia Neal, *The Art of Convening: Authentic Engagement in Meetings, Gatherings, and Conversations*

ABOUT THE AUTHOR

Richard E. Hinkie

Ric Hinkie has helped more than 400,000 individuals become more successful by helping them grow their work skills, knowledge and abilities. He has led teams that created job specific and general professional development tools for the United States Action Agency, the American Gas Association, the American Payroll Association, the Midwest Energy Association, the Society for Human Resource, Management along with Allied Signal, Carrier Corporation, Cutler-Hammer, the Urban Mass Transit Administration and numerous other national enterprises.

He is a former: utility executive; educational and career-development consultant to Fortune 1000 companies, the United States Government, and trade and professional associations; president of a trade association which helps its members enhance the safety and productivity of their employees, and, as a result, adds to the customer satisfaction of millions of its members' customers. He is also a retired United States Army officer.

He continues to seek out successful people in all walks of life, to capture their life lessons so that he can pass them on. He believes strongly in sharing those lessons so that future generations can build upon the past and move society forward, rather than having to re-learn what works in life by trial and error.

For more information on how to Fast Forward Your Career, go to www.successfulcareerdecisions.com.